Microsoft® PowerPoint® 2013:
Level 1 of 3

ALEC FEHL

Asheville-Buncombe Technical Community College

LABYRINTH
LEARNING™

Berkeley, CA

Microsoft PowerPoint 2013: Level 1

Copyright © 2014 by Labyrinth Learning

LABYRINTH
LEARNING™

Labyrinth Learning
2560 9th Street, Suite 320
Berkeley, California 94710
800.522.9746
On the web at lablearning.com

President:
Brian Favro

Product Development Manager:
Jason Favro

Managing Editor:
Laura Popelka

Production Editor:
Margaret Young

Production Manager:
Rad Proctor

eLearning Production Manager:
Arl S. Nadel

eLearning Development:
Judy Mardar and Andrew Vaughnley

Developmental Editors:
Trisha Conlon and Sandra Rittman

Indexing:
Joanne Sprott

Cover Design:
Mick Koller, SuperLab Design

Interior Design:
Mark Ong, Side-by-Side Studio

Labyrinth Learning™ and the Labyrinth Learning logo are trademarks of Labyrinth Learning. Microsoft® is a registered trademark of Microsoft Corporation in the United States and/or other countries and is used by Labyrinth Learning under license from owner. This title is an independent publication not affiliated with Microsoft Corporation. Other product and company names mentioned herein may be the trademarks of their respective owners.

The example companies, organizations, products, people, and events depicted herein are fictitious. No association with any real company, organization, product, person, or event is intended or inferred.

Screenshots reprinted with permission.

ITEM: 1-59136-494-9
ISBN-13: 978-1-59136-494-8

Manufactured in the United States of America.

10 9 8 7 6 5 4 3 2 1

Table of Contents

Quick Reference Tables

Preface

In today's digital world, knowing how to use the most popular suite of desktop software applications is critical. Our goal is to teach new users how to take advantage of this technology and to help experienced users understand how the applications have changed from previous versions. We begin with fundamental concepts and take learners through a systematic progression of exercises, resulting in skill mastery.

An online student resource center accompanies this book. It contains Concepts Review quizzes, student exercise files, and other learning tools. The URL for the student resource center is printed on the inside front cover of this textbook.

Supplemental Options

Video Tutorials: Our easy-to-follow instructional design is complemented with hundreds of videos that demonstrate the concepts and skills covered in this textbook. All videos can be accessed online with a single license key. Videos are an option for all learners. Keys can be purchased at http://lablearning.com/Store/Shop-Videos.

eLab Course Management System: eLab is a web-based learning systems that integrates seamlessly with this textbook. eLab is an option for students enrolled in instructor-led courses that have adopted eLab as part of their course curriculum.

Visual Conventions

This book uses visual and typographic cues to guide students through the lessons. Some of these cues are described below.

`Type this text`	Text you type at the keyboard is printed in this typeface.
Action words	The important action words in exercise steps are presented in boldface.
Ribbon	Glossary terms are presented in black text with a blue background.
TIP	Tips, notes, and warnings are called out with special icons.
Command→ Command→ Command→ Command	Commands to execute from the Ribbon are presented like this: Ribbon Tab→Command Group→Command→Subcommand.
FROM THE KEYBOARD Ctrl + S to save	These margin notes present shortcut keys for executing certain tasks.
FROM THE RIBBON File→Save	These margin notes show Ribbon paths for executing certain tasks.

Acknowledgements

This textbook has benefited greatly from the reviews and suggestions of the following instructors.

Ann Blackman, *Parkland College*

Lori Collins, *Pike-Lincoln Technical Center*

Rhonda Davis, *Isothermal Community College*

Miriam Foronda, *University of New Mexico – Taos*

Teresita Galvizo, *South East High School*

Joan Johnson, *Lake Sumter Community College*

John Mims, *Central New Mexico Community College Workforce Training Center*

Kay Nelson, *The Lifelong Learning Center, Missoula County Public Schools*

Monika Olsen, *Acalanes Adult Education*

Kari Phillips, *Davis Applied Technology College*

Mary Jo Slater, *Community College of Beaver County*

Cynthia Wade, *CierraTEC*

Microsoft® PowerPoint 2013:
Level 1 of 3

POWERPOINT 2013

Creating and Delivering a Presentation

LEARNING OBJECTIVES

After studying this lesson, you will be able to:

- Apply a document theme to a new presentation
- Insert new slides
- Add text to a slide
- View a slide show
- Present a slide show

In this lesson, you will create a PowerPoint presentation for the iJams music distribution company. Throughout the lesson, you will be using many PowerPoint features to develop the presentation. You will be working with document themes, text layout styles, and Microsoft Word outlines. By the end of the lesson, your presentation will be ready for delivery. Equipped with the tips and techniques for a successful presentation, you will practice its delivery to the JamWorks trade show.

Creating a Presentation

iJams is an online music distribution company that sells physical CDs in addition to downloadable music. Unsigned musicians send in an existing CD or MP3 files of their original material, and then iJams duplicates the CDs on demand as orders come in and makes the MP3s available for immediate purchase or download. Musicians can also send in digital files of CD artwork, and iJams will print full-color CD inserts and other supporting materials. Additionally, iJams sells promotional items such as T-shirts, stickers, and mouse pads branded for artists.

As an employee of iJams, you have been asked to make a presentation representing the company to the JamWorks trade show. Your goal is to introduce iJams to trade show attendees and entice them with a promotional offer. You decide to use PowerPoint with a new netbook computer and video projection system to develop and deliver your presentation. You choose PowerPoint because it is easy to learn and seamlessly integrates with other Microsoft Office applications.

Slides from the iJams presentation

Presenting PowerPoint

Video Library   http://labyrinthelab.com/videos   Video Number: PP13-V0101

PowerPoint 2013 is an intuitive, powerful presentation graphics program that enables you to create dynamic, multimedia presentations for a variety of functions. Whether you are developing a one-on-one presentation for your manager or a sophisticated presentation for a large group, PowerPoint provides the tools to make your presentation a success. PowerPoint allows you to project your presentation in a variety of ways. Most presentations are delivered via a computer projection display attached to a notebook computer. There are also other ways to deliver presentations. For example, you can deliver a presentation as an online broadcast over the Internet or save it as a video to be emailed or distributed on CD.

PowerPoint provides easy-to-use tools that let you concentrate on the content of your presentation instead of focusing on the design details. Using PowerPoint's built-in document themes, you can rapidly create highly effective professional presentations.

Starting PowerPoint

To create a new presentation, use one of the following methods.

- In Windows 7, click the Start button then choose All Programs→Microsoft Office 2013→PowerPoint 2013.
- In Windows 8, scroll to the right of the Start screen then click the PowerPoint 2013 tile.

After the PowerPoint program has started, click Blank Presentation to create a new blank presentation. To open an existing presentation:

- Start PowerPoint, choose File→Open and click a recent presentation, or navigate to the presentation file and double-click it.
- In either version of Windows, navigate to the desired presentation by using Windows Explorer or Computer and double-click the presentation.

Start PowerPoint

In this exercise, you will start PowerPoint.

1. Follow these steps for the version of Windows you are running to open the PowerPoint 2013 program:

Windows 7

Ⓐ Click **Start**.

Ⓑ Point to **All Programs**.

Ⓒ Scroll down if necessary.

Ⓓ Click **Microsoft Office 2013**.

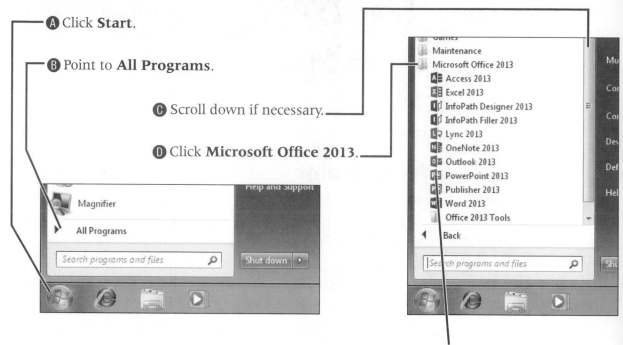

Ⓔ Click **PowerPoint 2013**.

Windows 8

Ⓐ Tap the [Windows] key, if necessary, to show the **Start screen**.

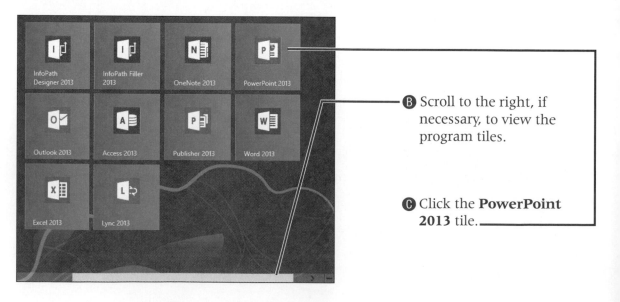

Ⓑ Scroll to the right, if necessary, to view the program tiles.

Ⓒ Click the **PowerPoint 2013** tile.

Creating a New Presentation

Video Library   http://labyrinthelab.com/videos   Video Number: PP13-V0102

When PowerPoint 2013 starts, it displays a Start screen that offers a variety of templates from which to choose. If your computer is connected to the Internet, PowerPoint will automatically display additional templates downloaded from the Microsoft web site. A template is a blank presentation that is preformatted with matching graphics, colors, and fonts. If you are not connected to the Internet, PowerPoint will display its default templates. A blank presentation option also is always available on the Start screen. Using the blank presentation template creates a blank, unformatted presentation to which you can add graphics, colors, and special fonts later.

Recently opened presentations are displayed here.

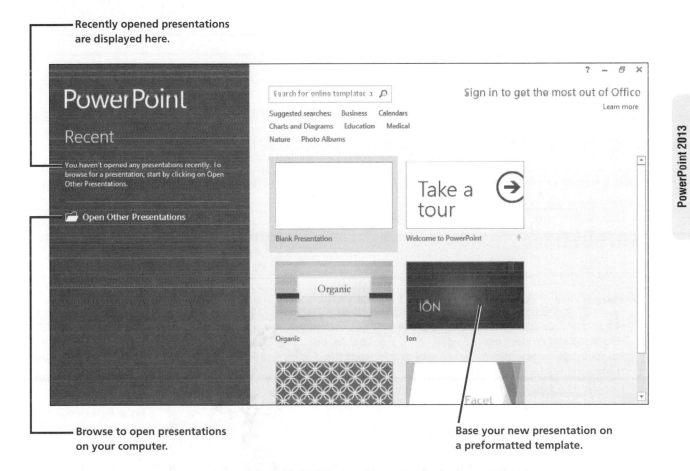

Browse to open presentations on your computer.

Base your new presentation on a preformatted template.

DEVELOP YOUR SKILLS PP01-D02
Create a Blank Presentation

In this exercise, you will create a new, blank presentation.

1. Click the **Blank Presentation** template on the PowerPoint Start screen.

   A new, blank presentation appears. You will develop it throughout this lesson.

Navigating the PowerPoint Window

The PowerPoint 2013 program window, like other Microsoft Office programs, groups commands on the Ribbon. The following illustration provides an overview of the program window.

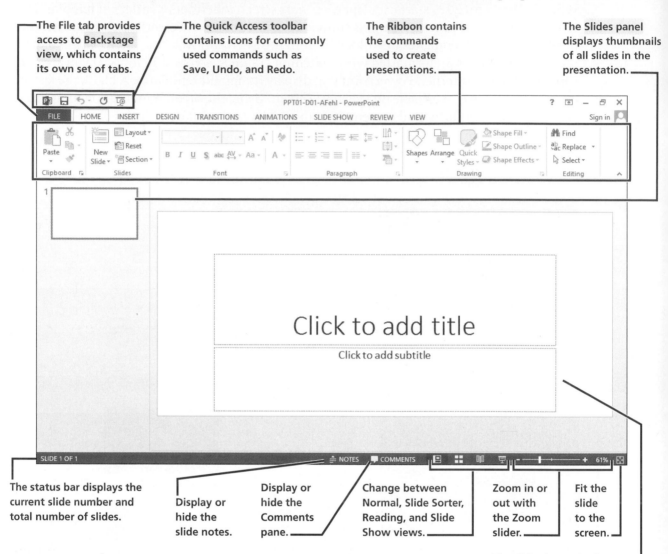

The File tab provides access to **Backstage** view, which contains its own set of tabs.

The Quick Access toolbar contains icons for commonly used commands such as Save, Undo, and Redo.

The Ribbon contains the commands used to create presentations.

The Slides panel displays thumbnails of all slides in the presentation.

The status bar displays the current slide number and total number of slides.

Display or hide the slide notes.

Display or hide the **Comments** pane.

Change between Normal, Slide Sorter, Reading, and Slide Show views.

Zoom in or out with the Zoom slider.

Fit the slide to the screen.

The slide chosen in the Slides panel is shown here.

Saving the Presentation

Video Library   http://labyrinthelab.com/videos   Video Number: PP13-V0103

The byword in PowerPoint is to save early and save often. You can use the Save button on the Quick Access toolbar or in Backstage view. If it's the first time a presentation has been saved, the Save As dialog box will appear because the file will need a name and location on your computer. You can also use the Save As dialog box to make a copy of a presentation by saving it under a new name or to a different location. If the file has already been saved, PowerPoint replaces the previous version with the new, edited version.

FROM THE KEYBOARD
Ctrl+S to save

FROM THE RIBBON
File→Save

Save the Presentation

In this exercise, you will save the presentation by giving it a name and a location on your computer.

Before You Begin: Navigate to the student resource center to download the student exercise files for this book.

1. Click the **Save** 🔲 button on the Quick Access toolbar.

PowerPoint displays the Save As dialog box because this presentation has not yet been given a filename.

2. Follow these steps to save the presentation to your file storage location:

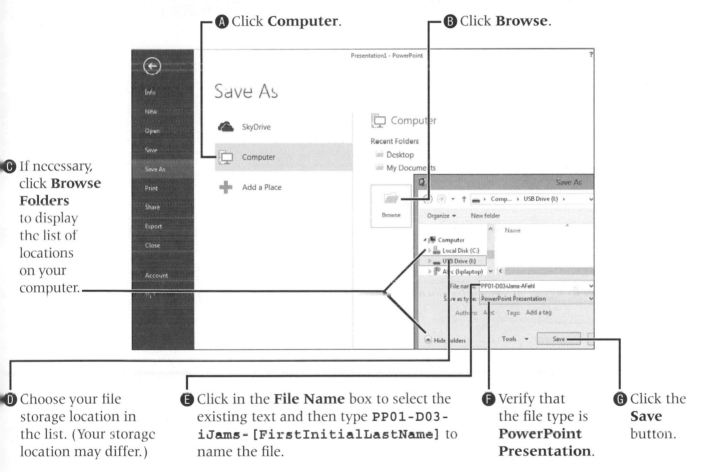

Ⓐ Click **Computer**.

Ⓑ Click **Browse**.

Ⓒ If necessary, click **Browse Folders** to display the list of locations on your computer.

Ⓓ Choose your file storage location in the list. (Your storage location may differ.)

Ⓔ Click in the **File Name** box to select the existing text and then type **PP01-D03-iJams-[FirstInitialLastName]** to name the file.

Ⓕ Verify that the file type is **PowerPoint Presentation**.

Ⓖ Click the **Save** button.

In the filename, replace the bracketed text with your first initial and last name. For example, the author's filename would look like this: PP01-D03-iJams-AFehl.

PowerPoint saves the presentation.

PowerPoint 2013

Save as Video

PowerPoint 2013 also allows you to save your presentation as a video. This is helpful if you want to distribute your presentation to others without requiring them to have PowerPoint or other special software. The video files are saved in the MPEG-4 (.mp4) format and are playable on any computer. When saving as a video, be patient as it takes some time to convert your presentation to the video format.

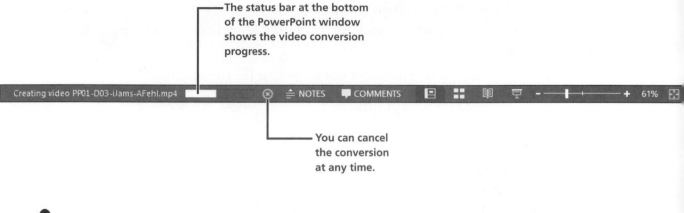

The status bar at the bottom of the PowerPoint window shows the video conversion progress.

You can cancel the conversion at any time.

The video version of a presentation can be 15 times larger than the original PowerPoint file. Be aware of the file size before you try to email a video to someone.

FROM THE RIBBON
File→Export→Create a Video

Inserting Text

Video Library   http://labyrinthelab.com/videos   Video Number: PP13-V0104

PowerPoint slides have placeholders set up for you to type in. For example, the title slide currently visible on the screen has placeholders for a title and subtitle. You click in the desired placeholder to enter text on a slide. For example, to enter the title on a slide, you click in the title placeholder and then type the text. Do not press the [Enter] key; the placeholders are already formatted with word wrap. The placeholders also are already formatted with font and paragraph settings to make a cohesive presentation. As you will see shortly, it's easy to make changes to the formatting of slides by applying a theme.

Type a Title Slide

In this exercise, you will enter a title and subtitle for the presentation.

1. Choose **File→Save As** and save your file as `PP01-D04-iJams-[FirstInitialLastName]`.

2. Follow these steps to add a title and subtitle:

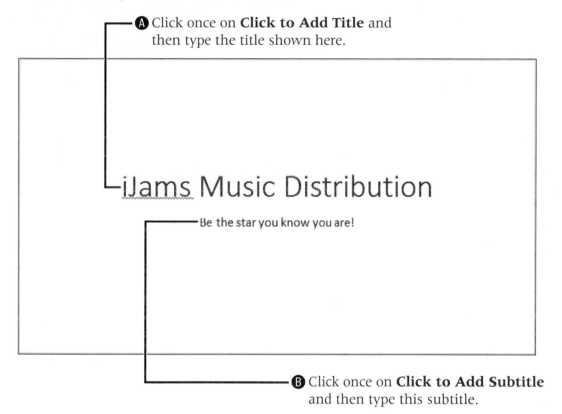

Ⓐ Click once on **Click to Add Title** and then type the title shown here.

iJams Music Distribution

Be the star you know you are!

Ⓑ Click once on **Click to Add Subtitle** and then type this subtitle.

PowerPoint enters the titles. At this point, you have a title slide, but it looks rather plain. This is about to change.

3. Save the presentation and leave it open; you will modify it throughout the lesson.

Using Document Themes

Video Library   http://labyrinthelab.com/videos   Video Number: PP13-V0105

You can use PowerPoint's built-in document themes, which provide a ready-made backdrop for your presentations, to easily format all slides in a presentation. When you use a document theme, your presentation automatically includes an attractive color scheme, consistent font style and size, and bulleted lists to synchronize with the design and style of the presentation. Document themes also position placeholders on slides for titles, text, bulleted lists, graphics, and other objects. By using document themes, you can focus on content by simply filling in the blanks as you create the presentation. You access document themes from the Themes group on the Design tab.

Choosing a Theme

NEW! 2013

Nine document themes are included with PowerPoint 2013. Additionally, each theme has four variations. A theme variation uses different colors and sometimes a different background. PowerPoint automatically downloads additional themes and adds them to the Themes gallery on the Ribbon if your computer is connected to the Internet. Match the theme to the type of presentation you are giving. Keep the design appropriate to the function and the audience.

This area displays the themes used in the current presentation.

Pointing over a thumbnail displays the theme temporarily on your slide. Click a thumbnail to apply the theme.

Theme variations are listed here.

Change the slide size from widescreen (16:9) to standard (4:3).

Find more themes or save a modified theme.

Right-click a thumbnail to show other theme options.

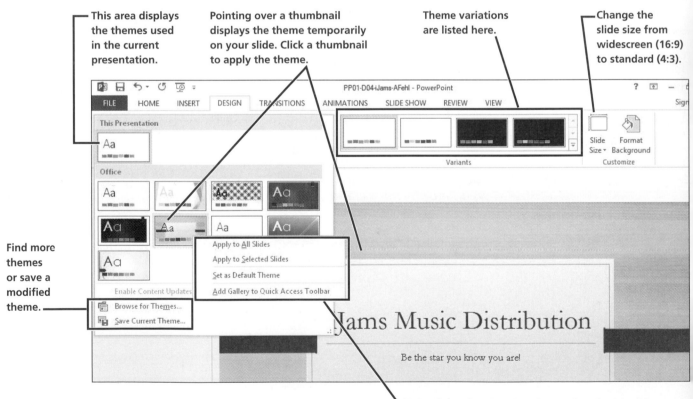

Finding Additional Themes

New themes are sent to Microsoft daily, so if you just can't find the right one, browse the Microsoft Office Online website for new themes. You can also search for new themes from the PowerPoint Start screen.

Using the PowerPoint Ribbon

The PowerPoint Ribbon is organized into nine default tabs: File, Home, Insert, Design, Transitions, Animations, Slide Show, Review, and View. As in other Office 2013 applications, additional tabs appear when certain elements on a slide are selected. These additional tabs, called contextual tabs, offer commands specific to the selected element; for example, selecting a picture on a slide results in the Picture Tools Format tab being shown. Deselecting the picture returns the Ribbon to its original state with the nine default tabs.

FROM THE RIBBON

Design→Themes

Each tab contains many commands, which are organized in groups called command groups. Each group is labeled across the bottom and contains a variety of buttons or button menus.

The Home tab displays several groups of buttons.

Some groups contain a small icon in the bottom-right corner that, when clicked, displays a dialog box or a task pane.

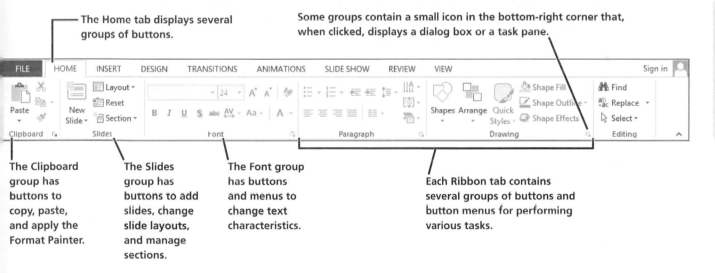

PowerPoint 2013

The Clipboard group has buttons to copy, paste, and apply the Format Painter.

The Slides group has buttons to add slides, change slide layouts, and manage sections.

The Font group has buttons and menus to change text characteristics.

Each Ribbon tab contains several groups of buttons and button menus for performing various tasks.

Apply a Document Theme

In this exercise, you will choose a document theme and apply it to the presentation.

1. Choose **File→Save As** and save your file as `PP01-D05-iJams-[FirstInitialLastName]`.

2. Follow these steps to choose a theme for the presentation:

    Depending on your monitor resolution, you may see a different number of thumbnails in the Themes group.

    Ⓐ Display the **Design** tab.

    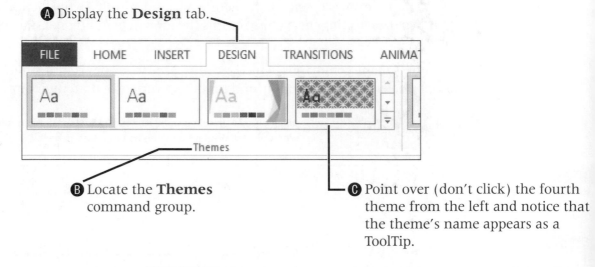

    Ⓑ Locate the **Themes** command group.

    Ⓒ Point over (don't click) the fourth theme from the left and notice that the theme's name appears as a ToolTip.

    PowerPoint displays a Live Preview of the theme on your title slide. This gives you a good idea of the overall design of the theme. Notice that the fonts and locations have changed for the title and subtitle. A different theme can radically redesign your presentation.

    Throughout this book, the preceding command will be written as follows: Choose Design→Themes→[Theme command].

3. Point over (don't click) several more theme thumbnails.

    You see a Live Preview of each theme on the actual slide. The themes visible on the Ribbon are just a small portion of those available, however.

4. Follow these steps to choose a theme:

Ⓐ Choose **Design→Themes→More**. Ⓑ Point to preview the **Organic** theme.

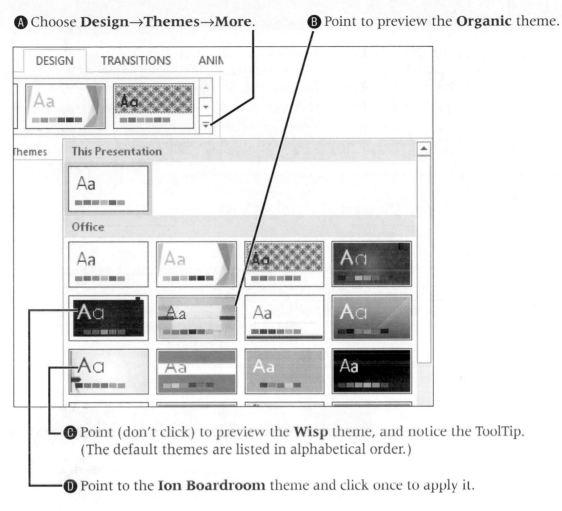

Ⓒ Point (don't click) to preview the **Wisp** theme, and notice the ToolTip. (The default themes are listed in alphabetical order.)

Ⓓ Point to the **Ion Boardroom** theme and click once to apply it.

PowerPoint applies the theme to your presentation.

5. Save the presentation and leave it open for the next exercise.

Choosing Slide Sizes

Video Library   http://labyrinthelab.com/videos   Video Number: PP13-V0106

By default, PowerPoint creates slides for widescreen format with a 16:9 ratio. This maximizes the use of space on the slide by taking advantage of the widescreen format on most modern computers. In fact, many of the new PowerPoint 2013 themes were designed specifically for widescreen use. You can easily switch to standard (4:3) format from the Ribbon if you need a narrower slide or have a non-widescreen computer monitor.

FROM THE RIBBON
Design→Customize →Slide Size to change the slide size

DEVELOP YOUR SKILLS PP01-D06
Apply a Theme Variation

In this exercise, you will experiment with slide sizes and choose a document theme variation.

1. Save your file as **PP01-D06-iJams-[FirstInitialLastName]**.

2. Follow these steps to change the slide size:

Ⓐ Display the **Design** tab.   **Ⓑ** Locate the **Customize** command group.   **Ⓒ** Click the **Slide Size** button.

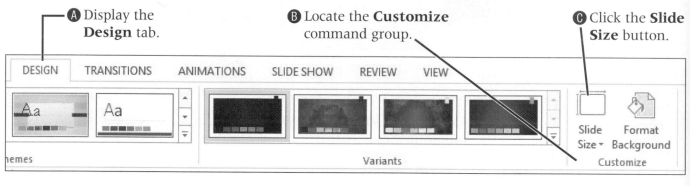

Ⓓ Click **Standard (4:3)**.

Ⓔ Click **Ensure Fit**.

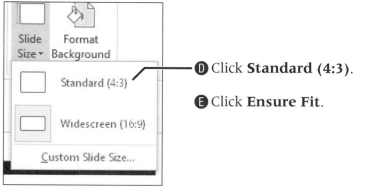

The slide is resized, and the slide title shifts to wrap across two lines.

3. Choose **Design→Customize→Slide Size→Widescreen (16:9)** to return the slide to widescreen format.

4. Locate the **Design→Variants** group on the Ribbon.

5. Point to several theme variations to view the Live Preview on the slide.

6. Click the **second variation** (with the green background) to apply it.

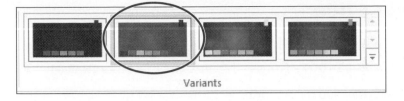

Variants

7. Save the presentation and leave it open for the next exercise.

Creating a Basic Presentation

Video Library   http://labyrinthelab.com/videos   Video Number: PP13-V0107

There is more to creating a presentation than placing one slide after another. Choosing the appropriate slide layout, just like choosing the appropriate design, will influence how well your audience understands your message. Use the following guidelines when choosing your slide design and layout:

■ **Know your audience:** Will you be speaking to accountants or artists?

■ **Know your purpose:** Are you introducing a product or giving a report?

■ **Know your expectations:** When the last word of this presentation has been given, how do you want your audience to respond to your facts? Are you looking for approval for a project or customers for a product?

Adding Slides

You can add slides to a presentation from the Ribbon or by right-clicking with the mouse. PowerPoint always places the new slide after the currently selected slide.

The Slides panel displays thumbnails of your presentation while you work in the Normal view. The Slide Sorter view, like the Slides panel, also displays thumbnails of your slides. This view can be useful when there are more slides than can fit in the Slides panel display.

QUICK REFERENCE	ADDING SLIDES
Task	**Procedure**
Add a slide with the Ribbon	■ Choose Home→Slides→New Slide 🖽.
Add a slide with the mouse	■ Right-click a slide on the Slides panel. ■ Choose New Slide from the pop-up (context) menu.

PowerPoint 2013

Add a New Slide

In this exercise, you will add a new slide to the presentation and then enter content.

1. Save your file as **PP01-D07-iJams-[FirstInitialLastName]**.

2. Follow these steps to add a new slide:

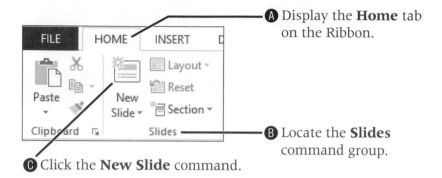

A Display the **Home** tab on the Ribbon.

B Locate the **Slides** command group.

C Click the **New Slide** command.

PowerPoint adds a new slide to the presentation immediately after the title slide.

3. Click once in the title placeholder and then type **Our Services** as the title.

4. Click once on the **Click to Add Text** placeholder and then type the following list. Tap the Enter key after each list item except the last one.

   - **CD duplication on demand** Enter
   - **Jewel-case-insert printing** Enter
   - **Full-service online sales** Enter
   - **Downloadable MP3 distribution**

   PowerPoint adds a bullet in front of each line.

5. Save the presentation and leave it open for the next exercise.

Duplicating a Slide

Sometimes it is more efficient to duplicate a slide and then edit it rather than begin a new slide from scratch. Slides can be duplicated via the Slides panel.

QUICK REFERENCE	DUPLICATING A SLIDE
Task	**Procedure**
Duplicate a single slide	▪ Right-click the slide you wish to duplicate in the Slides panel. ▪ Choose Duplicate Slide. The new slide is inserted below the original.
Duplicate multiple slides	▪ Use Ctrl+click or Shift+click to select the desired slides in the Slides panel. ▪ Right-click any of the selected slides and choose Duplicate Slide. The new slides are inserted below the selected slides.

Indenting Bulleted Lists

Video Library   http://labyrinthelab.com/videos   Video Number: PP13-V0108

When using PowerPoint, you can effortlessly create bulleted lists to outline the thrust of your presentation. The bulleted list layout is an outline of nine levels. A different indentation is used for each level. The following illustration shows the Packaging Options slide you will create in the next exercise.

This bulleted list has three levels. Each level uses the same shape character, but the text and bullet get smaller with each indentation.

Working with Bulleted Lists

When you use a document theme, each paragraph is automatically formatted as a bulleted list. The format includes a bullet style, indentation level, font type, and font size for each bulleted paragraph. This outline for the bulleted list is held within a placeholder or text box.

Working with List Levels

Indenting a bullet is referred to as demoting a bullet, or increasing the list level. Typically, a main bullet point has one or more sub-bullets. These sub-bullets, which are smaller than the main bullet, are created by increasing the list level. When a list level is increased, the bullets are indented toward the right. Conversely, decreasing a bullet's indent by moving it more toward the left and increasing the bullet size is referred to as promoting a bullet, or decreasing the list level. PowerPoint supports a main bullet and up to eight sub-bullets.

Task	Procedure
Turn bullets on and off	▪ Select the desired paragraph(s). ▪ Choose Home→Paragraph→Bullets ▤.
Promote bullets by using the Ribbon	▪ Select the desired paragraph(s). ▪ Choose Home→Paragraph→Decrease List Level ▤ or use ⌈Shift⌉+⌈Tab⌉.
Demote bullets by using the Ribbon	▪ Select the desired paragraph(s). ▪ Choose Home→Paragraph→Increase List Level ▤ or tap ⌈Tab⌉.

DEVELOP YOUR SKILLS PP01-D08
Create a Bulleted List

In this exercise, you will create a new slide and then enter information into a multilevel bulleted list.

1. Save your file as **PP01-D08-iJams-[FirstInitialLastName]**.

2. Choose **Home→Slides→New Slide** ▤.

   PowerPoint creates a new slide after the current slide.

3. Click in the title placeholder and type **Packaging Options**.

4. Click once in the text placeholder.

5. Type **CD labeling** and then tap ⌈Enter⌉.

   PowerPoint formats the new blank paragraph with the same large bullet. Paragraph formats are carried to new paragraphs when you tap the ⌈Enter⌉ key.

6. Tap ⌈Tab⌉.

   PowerPoint indents the paragraph. It also introduces a new, slightly smaller style for the level-2 paragraph.

7. Type **Full color**.

   PowerPoint formats the paragraph in a smaller font too.

8. Tap ⌈Enter⌉.

   PowerPoint maintains the same level-2 formatting for the next paragraph.

9. Type **Laser etching** and then tap ⌈Enter⌉.

10. While holding down ⌈Shift⌉, tap ⌈Tab⌉ once.

    PowerPoint promotes the new paragraph back to the level-1 style, which is the level of the first paragraph on the slide.

Manipulate Heading Levels

You can also adjust the level after you have typed a paragraph.

11. Type these lines:

- **Jewel case**
- **Back and spine of case**

12. Follow these steps to indent the last bullet:

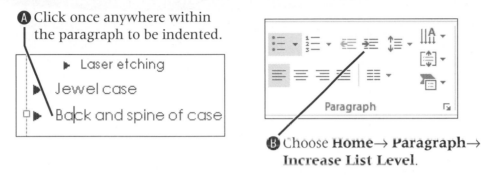

Ⓐ Click once anywhere within the paragraph to be indented.

Ⓑ Choose **Home→ Paragraph→ Increase List Level**.

PowerPoint indents the paragraph and changes the bullet style. Demoting a paragraph makes it subordinate to the preceding paragraph.

13. Click the **Increase List Level** button three more times.

The bullet and font sizes change with each level increase. These formats are determined by the Ion Boardroom theme, on which the presentation is based.

14. Click **Home→Paragraph→Decrease List Level** three times until the bullet reaches the second indentation.

With each promotion, the bullet style changes.

Indent Multiple Bullets

15. Click once at the end of the last paragraph and then tap Enter.

16. Type these new lines:

- **Insert**
- **Single sheet**
- **Up to 10-page booklet**

17. Follow these steps to select the last two paragraphs for your next command:

Ⓐ Point at the beginning of *Single sheet*, taking care that a four-pointed arrow is not visible.

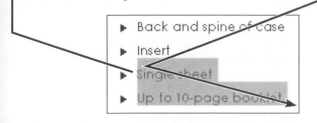

Ⓑ Drag down and right to select (highlight) to the end of the last paragraph; release the mouse button.

Ⓒ Ignore a Mini toolbar that appears. Take care not to click anywhere else on the slide before you perform the next step.

18. Choose **Home→Paragraph→Increase List Level**.

PowerPoint indents the two selected paragraphs.

19. Click anywhere outside the border to deselect the text. Your slide should match the following illustration.

Packaging Options

▶ CD labeling
  ▶ Full color
  ▶ Laser etching
▶ Jewel Case
  ▶ Back and spine of case
  ▶ Insert
    ▶ Single sheet
    ▶ Up to 10-page booklet

20. Save the presentation and leave it open for the next exercise.

Choosing the Slide Layout

Video Library   http://labyrinthelab.com/videos   Video Number: PP13-V0109

Slide layouts are named for the type of data they will contain. For example, the Title layout needs only a title and subtitle. The Content layout will hold other information on the slide, so it has a title and a bulleted list for points. Likewise, the Content with Caption layout is divided into three sections: title, text to one side, and an area for clip art or additional text. The slide layout organizes the information you put into the presentation by giving it a place on the slide. The new layout is applied to all selected slides. There are nine standard layouts, but many themes offer additional layouts.

FROM THE RIBBON
Home→Slides→
Layout ▼ menu

Clicking the Layout button in the Slides group on the Home tab allows you to apply a new layout to the selected slide(s).

Change the Slide Layout

In this exercise, you will add a new slide and then change its layout.

1. Save your file as **PP01-D09-iJams-[FirstInitialLastName]**.

2. If necessary, select the **Packaging Options** slide from the Slides panel on the left side of your screen.

3. Choose **Home→Slides→New Slide** 🖽.

   PowerPoint adds another slide to the end of the presentation. Like the previous two slides, this one is set up to display a bulleted list.

4. Follow these steps to choose a new layout for the slide:

   Ⓐ Choose **Home→Slides→Layout menu button.**▼

   Ⓑ Choose the **Section Header** slide layout.

PowerPoint applies the new layout. Now there are two placeholders, for a title and subtext.

5. Enter the following text:

- Title: **Questions?**
- Text: **End of our brief presentation**

Your slide should resemble the following illustration.

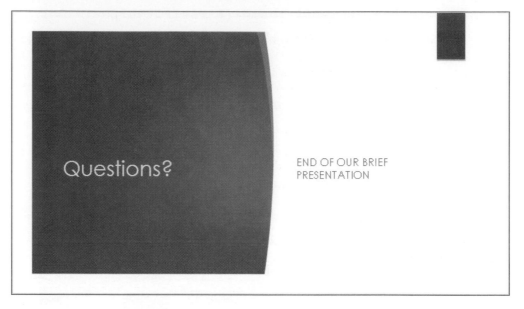

6. Save the presentation and leave it open for the next exercise.

Delivering the Slide Show

Video Library   http://labyrinthelab.com/videos   Video Number: PP13-V0110

The slides are created, and the presentation is complete. The first phase of the presentation development is over. The next phase, delivering the presentation, is just beginning. Before you stand before an audience, familiarize yourself with the following tips.

Delivery Tips

It is not only what you say, but how you say it that makes the difference between an engaging presentation and an unsuccessful one. Lead your audience. Help them to focus on the message of your presentation, not on you as the presenter. Use the following *PEER* guidelines to deliver an effective presentation:

- **Pace:** Maintain a moderate pace. Speaking too fast will exhaust your audience, and speaking too slowly may put them to sleep. Carry your audience with you as you talk.
- **Emphasis:** Pause for emphasis. As you present, use a brief pause to emphasize your point. This pause will give the audience time to absorb your message.

- **Eye contact:** Address your audience. Always face your audience while speaking. A common mistake is to speak while walking or facing the projection screen. Don't waste all of the work you have done in the presentation by losing the interest of your audience now. If you are speaking from a lectern or desk, resist the temptation to lean on it. Stand tall, make eye contact, and look directly at your audience.

- **Relax:** You are enthusiastic and want to convey that tone to the audience. However, when you speak, avoid fast movement, pacing, and rushed talking. Your audience will be drawn to your movements and miss the point. Remember that the audience is listening to you to learn; this material may be old hat to you, but it's new to them. So speak clearly, maintain a steady pace, and stay calm.

Navigating Through a Slide Show

You can use the mouse and/or simple keyboard commands to move through a slide show. These are the easiest ways to navigate from one slide to the next.

FROM THE KEYBOARD

Spacebar or → to advance a slide

Backspace or ← to back up a slide

The Slide Show Toolbar

The Slide Show toolbar is your navigator during the slide show. It is hidden when a slide show starts, but becomes visible when you move your mouse around or point to the lower-left area of the screen. The Slide Show toolbar can be used to navigate a slide show or to draw attention to a specific area on a slide. However, use of this toolbar is unnecessary when you present a simple slide show like this one.

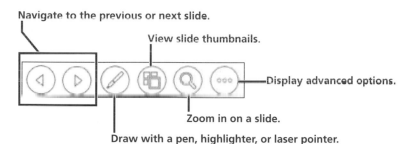

Navigate to the previous or next slide.

View slide thumbnails.

Display advanced options.

Zoom in on a slide.

Draw with a pen, highlighter, or laser pointer.

QUICK REFERENCE	USING BASIC SLIDE SHOW NAVIGATION
Task	**Procedure**
Advance a slide	▪ Click once with the mouse, or tap Spacebar, →, Page Down, or Enter.
Back up a slide	▪ Tap Backspace, Page Up, or ←.
Display the Slide Show toolbar	▪ Move the mouse around on the screen for a moment.

Run the Slide Show

In this exercise, you will navigate through your slide show.

1. Follow these steps to start the slide show:

    Ⓐ Click the title slide in the Slides panel to select it.

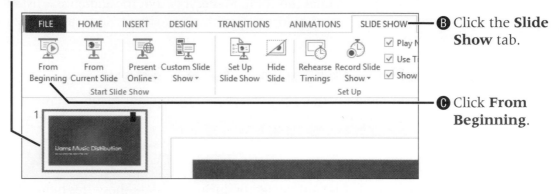

Ⓑ Click the **Slide Show** tab.

Ⓒ Click **From Beginning**.

2. Move the **mouse pointer** around the screen for a moment.

    Notice the Slide Show ◁ ▷ ⌀ ⊞ ⊕ ⊙ *toolbar that appears near the bottom-left corner of the screen when the slides are in full-screen view.*

3. Click the **mouse pointer** anywhere on the screen to move to the next slide.

4. Tap [Page Down] twice and then tap [Page Up] twice by using the keys near the main keyboard (not the keys on the numeric keypad).

    PowerPoint displays the next or previous slide each time you tap these keys.

5. Follow these steps to use the Slide Show toolbar:

    Ⓐ Point to the lower-left area of the slide to display the Slide Show toolbar.

    Ⓑ Click **Show all Slides** to display thumbnails of all slides.

6. Click the **Packaging Options** slide.

    As you can see, there are many ways to navigate slides in an electronic slide show.

End the Slide Show

7. Continue to click anywhere on the screen until the last slide appears (the Questions slide).

8. Click once on the last slide.

    The screen turns to a black background, with a small note at the top.

9. Click anywhere on the black screen to exit the slide show and return to the main PowerPoint window.

10. Feel free to practice running your slide show again.

11. Choose **File→Close** to close the presentation.

Getting Help

Video Library   http://labyrinthelab.com/videos   Video Number: PP13-V0111

PowerPoint, like many other software programs, has so many features that it is unlikely you will learn and remember everything about it at once. That is where PowerPoint Help comes in. You can use the help system to learn to perform specific tasks or browse general information about a variety of categories.

FROM THE KEYBOARD
F1

FROM THE RIBBON
Help ?

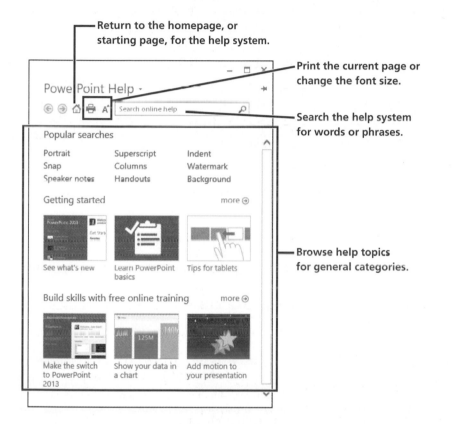

Return to the homepage, or starting page, for the help system.

Print the current page or change the font size.

Search the help system for words or phrases.

Browse help topics for general categories.

Using Online and Offline Help

If you are connected to the Internet when you open the PowerPoint Help window, PowerPoint connects to the Microsoft website and displays the most up-to-date help content. If you are not connected to the Internet, you can search for help topics in the offline help system that was installed on your computer when PowerPoint was installed.

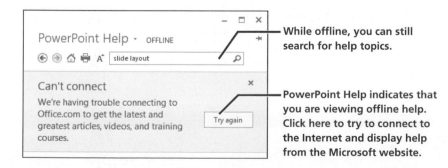

While offline, you can still search for help topics.

PowerPoint Help indicates that you are viewing offline help. Click here to try to connect to the Internet and display help from the Microsoft website.

PowerPoint 2013

Use PowerPoint Help

In this exercise, you will use the PowerPoint Help system.

1. Click the **Help** ? button on the right side of the Ribbon.

2. Follow these steps to search for help on a specific topic:

Ⓐ Click in the search box, type **slide layout**, and tap Enter.

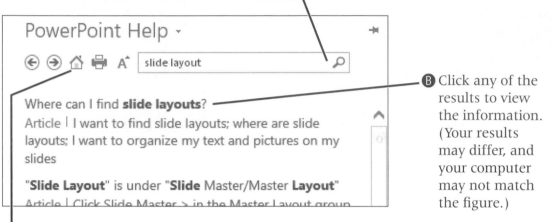

Ⓑ Click any of the results to view the information. (Your results may differ, and your computer may not match the figure.)

Ⓒ Click **Home** to return to the PowerPoint Help start page.

3. **Close** × the PowerPoint Help window.

4. Choose **File→Exit** to close PowerPoint.

Concepts Review

To check your knowledge of the key concepts introduced in this lesson, complete the Concepts Review quiz by choosing the appropriate access option below.

If you are...	Then access the quiz by...
Using the Labyrinth Video Library	Going to http://labyrinthelab.com/videos
Using eLab	Logging in, choosing Content, and navigating to the Concepts Review quiz for this lesson
Not using the Labyrinth Video Library or eLab	Going to the student resource center for this book

Reinforce Your Skills

Create a Presentation

In this exercise, you will begin to create a presentation for the Kids for Change organization—a community-based organization that helps socially aware youth plan and organize events that benefit their community. The presentation will be used to recruit new members and will be shown in high schools across the country.

Present PowerPoint

1. Start the **PowerPoint** program.

2. Click the **Blank Presentation** choice.

   A new presentation with a single slide is created.

3. **Save** the file as `PP01-R01-Kids-[FirstInitialLastName]` in the **PP2013 Lesson 01** folder.

4. Click the **Design** tab and familiarize yourself with the various commands there.

5. Click the **Home** tab and familiarize yourself with the various commands there.

Apply a Document Theme

6. Choose **Design→Themes** and then choose the **Facet** theme.

   PowerPoint applies the theme to your presentation.

7. Locate **Design→Variants** and then choose the second (the blue) variation.

   PowerPoint applies the color variation to your presentation.

8. Click in the **Title** placeholder and type the title `Kids for Change`.

9. Click in the **Subtitle** placeholder and type the subtitle `I can make a difference`.

   As you type, the text is automatically colored because that is a design element of this particular document theme.

10. Save and then close the presentation. Submit your final file based on the guidelines provided by your instructor. Exit **PowerPoint**.

    To view examples of how your file or files should look at the end of this exercise, go to the student resource center.

Add Slides and Deliver a Presentation

In this exercise, you will complete the Kids for Change presentation by adding slides and text. Finally, you will deliver the presentation and learn how to find help in PowerPoint.

Create a Basic Presentation

1. Start **PowerPoint**; open **PP01-R02-Kids** from the **PP2013 Lesson 01** folder and save it as `PP01-R02-Kids-[FirstInitialLastName]`.

2. Choose **Home→Slides→New Slide** 📄.

   A single-column, bulleted list slide is added to the presentation. Notice that the Facet document theme is applied to the new slide.

3. Choose **Home→Slides→** 📄 Layout ▾ **→Two Content**.

   A new, two-column layout is applied to the slide.

4. Click in the **Title** placeholder and type the title `Events`.

5. Add the following text to the bulleted list on the left:

   - `iRecycling Day`
   - `Toy Collection`
   - `Shave and a Haircut`
   - `Diversity Festival`

6. Add the following text to the bulleted list on the right:

   - `Build-a-House`
   - `Bully No More`
   - `Adopt a Street`
   - `Tutoring`

7. Save 💾 your presentation.

Create the Remaining Slides

8. Choose **Home→Slides→New Slide** 📄.

   A third slide is added to the presentation. The new slide has the same Two Content layout as the previous slide.

9. In the **Title** placeholder, enter the phrase **Program Benefits**.

10. In the first bullet of the left bulleted list, type **Personal** and tap ⌗Enter⌗.

11. Choose **Home→Paragraph→Increase List Level** 📑.

    The bullet is indented, and a new smaller bullet character is applied by the design template.

12. Add the following text to the bulleted list on the left:

    - **College application**
    - **Leadership skills**
    - **Sense of accomplishment**

13. In the first bullet of the bulleted list on the right, type **Community** and tap ⌗Enter⌗.

14. Choose **Home→Paragraph→Increase List Level** 📑.

    The bullet is indented, and a new smaller bullet character is applied by the design template.

15. Add the following text to the bulleted list on the right:

    - **Crime reduction**
    - **Increased literacy**
    - **Improved health**

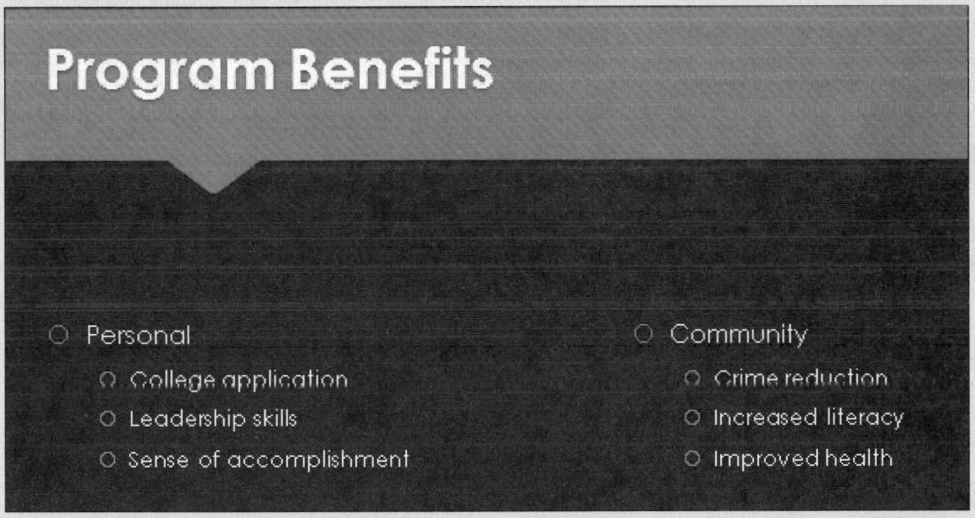

16. Choose **Home→Slides→New Slide** 📄.

17. Choose **Home→Slides→ 📄 Layout ▾ →Title and Content**.

18. Type the title `Requirements`.

19. Type the following bullet points in the text box:
    - `You need`
    - `Positive attitude`
    - `Strong work ethic`
    - `Time commitment`
    - `One monthly event`
    - `One annual meeting`

20. Select the *Positive attitude* and *Strong work ethic* paragraphs and increase their list level.

21. Select the *One monthly event* and *One annual meeting* paragraphs and increase their list level.

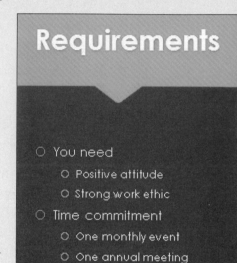

22. Choose **Home→Slides→New Slide**.

23. Type `Regional Contact` for the title.

24. Type the following in the text box:
    - `Angelica Escobedo`
    - `(800) 555-1212`

25. Click the **dashed border** around the text box so it turns solid, and then choose **Home→Paragraph→Bullets** to remove the bullets.
    The bullets are removed from all paragraphs in the text box.

26. Choose **Home→Paragraph→Center** to center the text on the slide.

Deliver a Slide Show

27. Select the first slide from the **Slides** panel on the left side of your screen.

28. Choose **Slide Show→Start Slide Show→From Beginning**.
    The title slide will occupy your whole screen as the slide show starts.

29. Walk through the presentation by clicking each slide until the presentation is ended.

30. Click once more to return to the PowerPoint program window.

31. Choose **Slide Show→Start Slide Show→From Beginning**  to start the slide show again.

32. After the slide show begins, position the mouse pointer at the bottom-left corner of the screen to display the **Slide Show** toolbar.

33. Click the **Show all Slides** button on the Slide Show toolbar.

    You will see thumbnails of each slide.

34. Click the **Program Benefits** slide.

35. Position the mouse pointer at the bottom-left corner of the screen to display the Slide Show toolbar.

36. Click the **More** button on the Slide Show toolbar.

37. Click **End Show** on the pop-up menu to end the slide show.

38. Save the presentation.

Find Help in PowerPoint

39. Click the **Help** button at the top-right of the Ribbon.

40. Type `customize theme` in the search box and then tap Enter.

41. Click the first result shown in the Help window and then read the help topic.

42. Close the **Help window** and exit **PowerPoint**.

43. Submit your final file based on the guidelines provided by your instructor. Exit **PowerPoint**.

    To view examples of how your file or files should look at the end of this exercise, go to the student resource center.

PowerPoint 2013

REINFORCE YOUR SKILLS PP01-R03

Create and Deliver a Presentation

In this exercise, you will create a presentation for Kids for Change that promotes their special event of the month.

Present PowerPoint

1. Start the **PowerPoint** program.

2. Click the **Blank Presentation** choice.

    A new presentation with a single slide is created.

3. Save 🖫 your file as `PP01-R03-Kids-[FirstInitialLastName]` in the **PP2013 Lesson 01** folder.

Apply a Document Theme

4. Choose **Design→Themes→More** and then choose the **Slice** theme.
   PowerPoint applies the theme to your presentation.

5. Locate **Design→Variants** and then choose the fourth variation.
   PowerPoint applies the variation to your presentation.

6. Click in the **Title** placeholder and type the title `Kids for Change`.

7. Click in the **Subtitle** placeholder and type the subtitle `June Event`.
   As you type, the text is automatically colored because that is a design element of this particular document theme.

8. Save 🖫 your presentation.

Create a Basic Presentation

9. Choose **Home→Slides→New Slide** 📄.

10. Click in the **Title** placeholder and type the title `Shave and a Haircut`.

11. Add the following text to the bulleted list:
    - `Free haircuts`
    - `Free shaves`
    - `Free mustache and beard trimming`

12. Save your presentation.

Create the Remaining Slides

13. Choose **Home→Slides→New Slide** 📄.

14. Choose **Home→Slides→** 📄 Layout ▾ **→Two Content**.
    A new two-column layout is applied to the slide.

15. In the **Title** placeholder, type `Participating Locations`.

16. In the first bullet of the left bulleted list, type `Barbers` and tap [Enter].

17. Choose **Home→Paragraph→Increase List Level** 📄.

18. Add the following text to the bulleted list on the left:
    - `Sam the Barber`
    - `Hats Off`
    - `Clean Cuts`

19. In the first bullet of the bulleted list on the right, type `Shelters` and tap [Enter].

20. Choose **Home→Paragraph→Increase List Level** 📄.
    The bullet is indented, and a new smaller bullet character is applied by the design theme.

21. Add the following text to the bulleted list on the right:
    - `Shelter on Main`
    - `Helping Hand`
    - `Safe Night`

22. Choose **Home**→**Slides**→**New Slide** 📄.

23. Choose **Home**→**Slides**→📄 Layout ▾ →**Title and Content**.

24. Enter the title `Dates and Availability`.

25. Type the following bullet points in the text box:
    - `All Locations`
    - `Every Saturday in June`
    - `8:00am - 8:00pm`
    - `Availability`
    - `Free service to help our community's homeless`

26. Select the two paragraphs under **All Locations** and increase their list level.

27. Select the last paragraph and increase its list level.

28. Choose **Home**→**Slides**→**New Slide** to add the final slide to the presentation.

29. Type `Sponsored By` for the title.

30. Type the following in the text box:
    - `Kids for Change`

31. Click the dashed border around the text box so it turns solid, and then choose **Home**→**Paragraph**→**Bullets** to remove the bullets.
    The bullets are removed from all paragraphs in the text box.

32. Choose **Home**→**Paragraph**→**Center** 📄 from the Ribbon to center the text on the slide.

Deliver a Slide Show

33. Select the first slide from the **Slides** panel on the left side of your screen.

34. Choose **Slide Show**→**Start Slide Show**→**From Beginning** 📄 from the Ribbon.
    The Title slide will occupy your whole screen as the slide show starts.

35. Walk through the presentation by clicking each slide until the presentation is ended.

36. Click once more to return to the PowerPoint program window.

37. Choose **Slide Show**→**Start Slide Show**→**From Beginning** 📄 from the Ribbon to start the slide show again.

38. After the slide show begins, position the mouse pointer at the bottom-left corner of the screen to display the **Slide Show** toolbar.

39. Click the **Show all Slides** button on the **Slide Show toolbar**.

40. Click the **Participating Locations** slide.

41. Position the mouse pointer at the bottom-left corner of the screen to display the **Slide Show toolbar**.

42. Click the **More** button on the Slide Show toolbar.

43. Click **End Show** on the pop-up menu to end the slide show.

44. Save the presentation.

Find Help in PowerPoint

45. Click the **Help** button at the top-right of the Ribbon.

46. Type `save movie` in the search box and then tap Enter.

47. Click the first result shown in the Help window and then read the help topic.

48. Close the **Help window** and exit **PowerPoint**.

49. Submit your final file based on the guidelines provided by your instructor.

Apply Your Skills

Create a Presentation

In this exercise, you will begin to create a presentation for Universal Corporate Events, a meeting and event planning service that handles event planning for businesses.

Start PowerPoint and Apply a Theme to a New Presentation

1. Start **PowerPoint**; create a new, blank presentation named **PP01-A01-Events-[FirstInitialLastName]** in the **PP2013 Lesson 01** folder.

2. Apply the **Facet** design document theme.

3. Apply the fourth variation, as shown in the illustration at the end of the exercise.

4. Add the following text to the title slide:
   - Title: **Universal Corporate Events**
   - Subtitle: **Events made easy**

5. Save your presentation. Exit **PowerPoint**.

6. Submit your final file based on the guidelines provided by your instructor.
   To view examples of how your file or files should look at the end of this exercise, go to the student resource center.

Add Slides and Deliver a Slide Show

In this exercise, you will complete the Universal Corporate Events presentation and deliver a slide show. Finally, you will have an opportunity to find help in PowerPoint.

Add Slides to a Presentation

1. Start **PowerPoint**; open **PP01-A02-Events** from the **PP2013 Lesson 01** folder and save it as **PP01-A02-Events-[FirstInitialLastName]**.

2. Add a second slide with the following text:

Title	Event Types
Bulleted paragraphs	■ Celebrations
	■ Team building
	■ Tradeshows
	■ Ceremonies

3. Add a third slide with the following text:

Title	Services
Bulleted paragraphs	■ Venue scouting
	■ Catering
	■ Invitations
	■ Stage and sound equipment

4. Add a fourth slide and change its layout to a **Two Content** layout. Add the following text:

Title	Benefits
Left bulleted paragraphs	■ Our jobs
	■ Deal with paperwork
	■ Guarantee safety
	■ Scheduling
Right bulleted paragraphs	■ Your jobs
	■ Relax
	■ Enjoy your event

5. Select all but the first bullet in the left text box and increase the list level.

6. Select all but the first bullet in the right text box and increase the list level.

7. Add a final slide to the presentation and apply the **Section Header** layout.
   - ■ Title: Universal Corporate Events
   - ■ Text: Events made easy

Deliver a Slide Show

8. Select the first slide from the **Slides** panel on the left side of your screen.

9. Start the slide show from the beginning.

10. Advance to the second slide.

11. Use the Slide Show toolbar to display all the slides and then jump to the **Benefits** slide.

12. Continue navigating the slides until the slide show ends and you are returned to the main PowerPoint window.

13. Save the presentation.

Get Help in PowerPoint

14. Start **Help** and search for clear text formatting.

15. Read the first help topic and then close the Help window.

16. Exit **PowerPoint**.

17. Submit your final file based on the guidelines provided by your instructor.

    To view examples of how your file or files should look at the end of this exercise, go to the student resource center.

Create and Deliver a Presentation

In this exercise, you will create a new presentation for Universal Corporate Events that outlines each of their services.

1. Start **PowerPoint**.

2. Click **Blank Presentation**.

   A new presentation with a single slide is created.

3. Save your file as **PP01-A03-Events-[FirstInitialLastName]** in the **PP2013 Lesson 01** folder.

Apply a Document Theme

4. Apply the **Retrospect** theme.

   PowerPoint applies the theme to your presentation.

5. Locate **Design→Variants** and then choose the third variation.

6. Click in the **Title** placeholder and type the title **Universal Corporate Events**.

7. Click in the **Subtitle** placeholder and type the subtitle **Services**.

8. Save your presentation.

Add Slides to a Presentation

9. Add a second slide with the following text:

Title	Venue Scouting
Bulleted paragraphs	■ Locate three potential venues
	■ Provide digital tour
	■ Provide transportation for up to four

10. Add a third slide with the following text:

Title	Catering
Bulleted paragraphs	■ Vegetarian and vegan options
	■ Kosher options
	■ Never frozen

11. Add a fourth slide and change its layout to a **Two Content** layout. Add the following text:

Title	Invitations
Left bulleted paragraphs	■ Creative ■ Graphic design ■ Matching envelopes
Right bulleted paragraphs	■ Business ■ Create mailing labels ■ Mail first class

12. Select all but the first bullet in the left text box and increase the list level.

13. Select all but the first bullet in the right text box and increase the list level.

14. Add a final slide to the presentation. Apply the **Title and Content** layout and add the following text:

Title	Stage and Sound Equipment
Bulleted paragraphs	■ Speaker podium and PA ■ 1200 watt sound system for bands ■ Portable dance floor

Deliver a Slide Show

15. Select the first slide from the **Slides** panel on the left side of your screen.

16. Start the slide show from the beginning.

17. Advance to the second slide.

18. Use the Slide Show toolbar to display all the slides and then jump to the **Catering** slide.

19. Continue navigating the slides until the slide show ends and you are returned to the main PowerPoint window.

20. Save the presentation.

Get Help in PowerPoint

21. Start **Help** and search for `insert YouTube video`.

22. Read the first help topic and then close the Help window.

23. Exit **PowerPoint**.

24. Submit your final file based on the guidelines provided by your instructor.

Extend Your Skills

In the course of working through the Extend Your Skills exercises, you will think critically as you use the skills taught in the lesson to complete the assigned projects. To evaluate your mastery and completion of the exercises, your instructor may use a rubric, with which more points are allotted according to performance characteristics. (The more you do, the more you earn!) Ask your instructor how your work will be evaluated.

PP01-E01 That's the Way I See It

You are creating a presentation for a charity that you feel strongly about in order to educate others about it. First, decide on a known charity you support or agree with. If you don't know of any charities, think of a few ideas for charities (such as saving animals or the environment, ensuring human rights, curing disease, etc.). Then, use the Internet to find a reputable charity that deals with one of those topics.

Create a new, blank presentation and save it as **PP01-E01-Charity-[FirstInitialLastName]** in the **PP2013 Lesson 01** folder. Apply the design theme and variation of your choice. Type the charity name as the slide title and type a short, descriptive phrase for the subtitle. Add a Title and Content slide that lists at least four actions the charity takes toward bettering their cause. Add a Two Content slide. On the left, list a few facts about the charity. On the right, list ways to donate to the charity. Create a final slide with the Section Header layout that duplicates the content shown on the title slide. View the presentation as a slide show and make a mental note of anything you want to change. When the slide show ends, make your changes and then save your presentation.

You will be evaluated based on the inclusion of all elements specified, your ability to follow directions, your ability to apply newly learned skills to a real-world situation, your creativity and the relevance of your topic and/or data choice(s). Submit your final file based on the guidelines provided by your instructor.

PP01-E02 Be Your Own Boss

Your landscaping business, Blue Jean Landscaping, saves its customers money by having them share in the physical labor. In this exercise, you will create multiple slides with varying layouts and bulleted text to advertise your unique business to potential investors. To begin, create a new, blank presentation named **PP01-E02-BlueJean-[FirstInitialLastName]** and saved to the **PP2013 Lesson 01** folder.

Apply the desired design theme and variation. Use the company name as the slide title and create a catchy phrase for the subtitle. Add a Title and Content slide that lists four services your company provides. Add a Two Content slide that lists the mutual benefits to the company and the customer: the left column uses **Us** as the first bullet, and the right column uses **You** as the first bullet. Then list at least three benefits for the company (left) and at least three for the customer (right). Increase the list level of all bullets except the first in each column.

Create a final slide with the Section Header layout that duplicates the content on the title slide. Run the slide show. Use the Slide Show toolbar to navigate the slide show and experiment with the other buttons on the toolbar. When the presentation ends, close PowerPoint. You will be evaluated based on the inclusion of all elements specified, your ability to follow directions, your ability to apply newly learned skills to a real-world situation, your creativity, and your demonstration of an entrepreneurial spirit. Submit your final file based on the guidelines provided by your instructor.

Transfer Your Skills

In the course of working through the Transfer Your Skills exercises, you will use critical-thinking and creativity skills to complete the assigned projects using skills taught in the lesson. To evaluate your mastery and completion of the exercises, your instructor may use a rubric, with which more points are allotted according to performance characteristics. (The more you do, the more you earn!) Ask your instructor how your work will be evaluated.

PP01-T01 Use the Web as a Learning Tool

Throughout this book, you will be provided with an opportunity to use the Internet as a learning tool by completing WebQuests. According to the original creators of WebQuests, as described on their website (WebQuest.org), a WebQuest is "an inquiry-oriented activity in which most or all of the information used by learners is drawn from the web." To complete the WebQuest projects in this book, navigate to the student resource center and choose the WebQuest for the lesson on which you are currently working. The subject of each WebQuest will be relevant to the material found in the lesson.

WebQuest Subject: Compare Presentation Graphics Software.

Submit your final file(s) based on the guidelines provided by your instructor.

PP01-T02 Demonstrate Proficiency

Stormy BBQ, a restaurant featuring fresh, locally grown vegetables and local, farm-raised pork/beef, is considering expanding to new locations. Create a PowerPoint presentation to show at a local town hall meeting to convince the local residents and community leaders that Stormy BBQ would be a great fit for their community.

Use an appropriate theme for the business and its commitment to the community. Perhaps search for additional themes from the PowerPoint Start screen. Create at least five slides, including the title slide, with a different layout for each slide. At least one slide should include bullet points with varying list levels.

Save the file as **PP01-T02-Stormy-[FirstInitialLastName]** to the **PP2013 Lesson 01** folder. Submit your final file based on the guidelines provided by your instructor.

Designing the Presentation

LEARNING OBJECTIVES

After studying this lesson, you will be able to:

- Use Outline view to create, move, and delete slides and edit text

- Create a presentation from a Microsoft Word outline

- Format and align text and adjust character spacing and line spacing

- Use Slide Sorter view and Sections

- Print a presentation

In this lesson, you will build on the fundamental design of the iJams presentation. To add professional credibility and make your presentation easier for an audience to follow, you will establish a consistent style throughout the presentation and format and organize the text. You will add from the Outline panel and organize your completed presentation by using Slide Sorter view and Sections. To quickly create a basic presentation, you will import a Microsoft Word outline. Finally, working with the printing function of PowerPoint 2013, you will examine page setup, print preview, print setup, and the output format options.

Designing a Presentation

Now that the initial slides of the iJams presentation are complete, you need to make sure that the style is consistent throughout the presentation. A consistent style appears more organized, is easier for an audience to follow, and adds professional credibility. You must also ensure that the slides are in a logical sequence so the presentation is clear.

Products and Promotional Items

- ▶ Audio CDs
- ▶ Downloadable MP3s
- ▶ T-shirts
- ▶ Baseball caps
- ▶ Stickers

- ▶ Pencils
- ▶ Key chains
- ▶ Posters
- ▶ Mugs
- ▶ Mouse pads

Sample of slide formatted with a layout Microsoft calls Two Content

Working with Slides

Video Library   http://labyrinthelab.com/videos   Video Number: PP13-V0201

As your presentation progresses and you insert additional slides, you may want to change the slide layout or order. For example, some slides may require two columns of bulleted text while others require only one. PowerPoint makes it easy to change the order of slides by using Slide Sorter view.

Copying Text and Objects

FROM THE RIBBON
Home→Clipboard→Cut
Home→Clipboard→Copy
Home→Clipboard→Paste

FROM THE KEYBOARD
Ctrl+X to cut
Ctrl+C to copy
Ctrl+V to paste

You can move and copy text and objects by using drag and drop or the Cut, Copy, and Paste commands. It is usually most efficient to use drag and drop if you are moving or copying text or objects within a slide. Drag and drop is also effective for rearranging slides. Cut, Copy, and Paste are most efficient when moving or copying to a location not visible on the current screen.

QUICK REFERENCE	MOVING AND COPYING TEXT AND OBJECTS
Task	**Procedure**
Drag and drop	■ Select the desired text or click an object (e.g., placeholder box).
	■ Drag the text/object to the desired location. Press Ctrl while dragging to copy.
Right-drag and drop	■ Select the desired text or click an object (e.g., placeholder box).
	■ Use the right mouse button to drag the text/object to the desired location.
	■ Release the mouse button at the desired location and choose Move, Copy, or Cancel.

DEVELOP YOUR SKILLS PP02-D01
Add a New Slide to a Presentation

In this exercise, you will add a new slide to a presentation, enter a bulleted list, and change the layout of the slide. You can always change the layout for a slide after the slide has been created.

1. Start **PowerPoint**. Open **PP02-D01-Design** from the **PP2013 Lesson 02** folder and save it as **PP02-D01-Design-[FirstInitialLastName]**.

   Replace the bracketed text with your first initial and last name. For example, if your name is Bethany Smith, your filename will look like this: PP02-D01-Design-BSmith.

2. Select the **Our Services** slide from the **Slides** panel on the left side of your screen.

   The Our Services slide appears. New slides are inserted after the selected slide.

3. Choose **Home→Slides→New Slide** 🗔.

4. Click in the **Title placeholder** and type **Products and Promotional Items**.

PowerPoint 2013 (side tab)

5. Click in the **bulleted list placeholder** and type this list:

- Audio CDs
- Downloadable MP3s
- T-shirts
- Baseball caps
- Stickers
- Pencils
- Key chains
- Posters
- Mugs
- Mouse pads

When you begin typing Mugs, *PowerPoint reformats the bullets with a smaller font size so they all fit in the box. As you type the last bullet point, the font gets even smaller. A long list of bullets can be overwhelming, so strive for no more than six bullets. If there is more information, consider breaking the list into two columns. You will use this technique next by choosing a different layout for the slide.*

6. Follow these steps to change the slide layout:

Ⓐ Display the **Home** tab.

Ⓑ Click the **Layout** menu ▼.

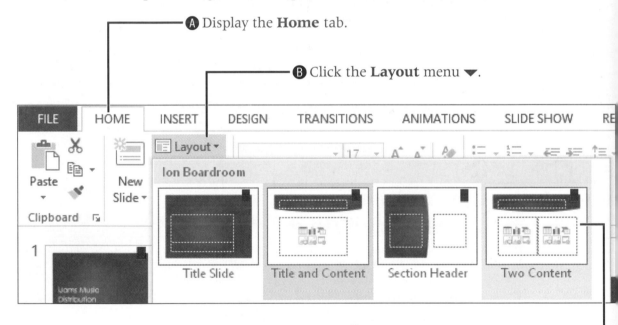

Ⓒ Choose the **Two Content** layout.

PowerPoint applies the Two Content layout to the current slide.

7. Follow these steps to move the last five bullets to the second box:

A Select the last five bulleted paragraphs.

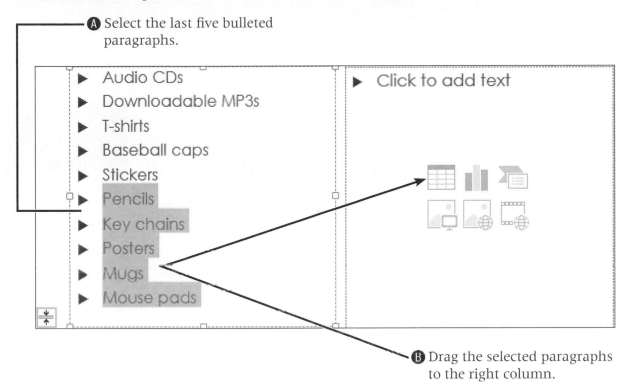

B Drag the selected paragraphs to the right column.

This action moves the last five bulleted paragraphs into the right-side content area.

8. Save ⊟ the changes to your presentation.

Working with Outlines

Video Library   http://labyrinthelab.com/videos   Video Number: PP13-V0202

Although you have been working primarily in the slide to add or format text, the Outline panel is an alternative way to add, remove, and move text. The Outline panel is a useful interface to organize and structure your presentation.

Using the Outline Panel

The Outline panel helps you edit and reorganize slides. It's available on the left side of the screen in Outline view. You can type directly in the Outline panel to add or edit text on a slide. You can also select text from the Outline panel and format it with the standard Ribbon formatting commands. Any changes made in the Outline panel are immediately reflected in the actual slide.

Switch to the Outline panel here.

The slide selected here is displayed in the main portion of the window.

Expand and collapse text content by double-clicking a slide icon.

Content of left and right content boxes of a two-column layout is indicated by the boxes 1 and 2.

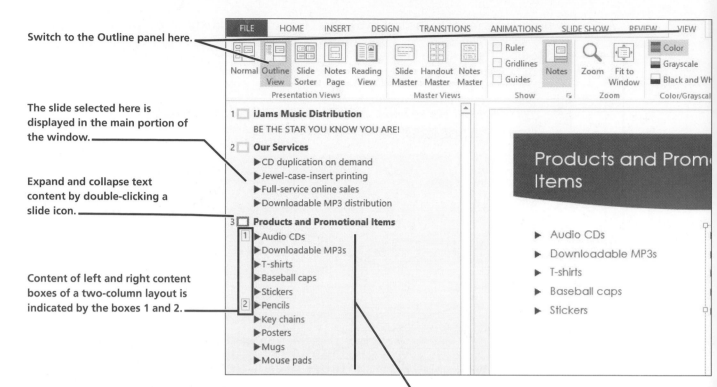

You can edit text directly on the Outline panel.

QUICK REFERENCE	WORKING WITH OUTLINES
Task	**Procedure**
Select text in an outline	Drag over the desired text in the Outline panel.
Select an entire slide	Click the slide icon in the Outline panel.
Expand or collapse a slide	Double-click the slide icon in the Outline panel. Right-click the slide text in the Outline panel and choose Collapse (All) or Expand (All).
Add a new slide	Place the mouse pointer in the last group of bulleted paragraphs on a slide and press Ctrl+Enter.
Delete a slide	Right-click any text within a slide in the Outline panel and choose Delete Slide.

Add a Slide in the Outline Panel

In this exercise, you will work with the Outline panel to add text.

1. Save your file as **PP02-D02-Design-[FirstInitialLastName]**.

2. Follow these steps to select a slide while in the Outline panel:

A Click the **View** tab.

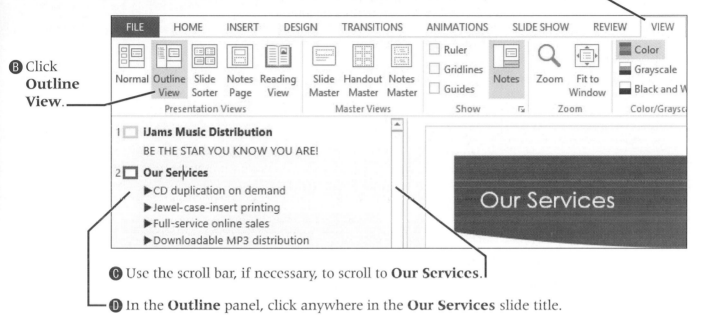

B Click **Outline View**.

C Use the scroll bar, if necessary, to scroll to **Our Services**.

D In the **Outline** panel, click anywhere in the **Our Services** slide title.

3. Press Ctrl + Enter.
   The insertion point moves to the first bulleted paragraph in the slide.

4. Press Ctrl + Enter again.
   PowerPoint creates a new slide below the selected slide.

5. Follow these steps to add text to the new slide while in the Outline panel:

Ⓐ Type **Current Artists** here. Notice that the text also appears in the main portion of your window.

Ⓑ Press Ctrl + Enter to move to the first bulleted paragraph.

Ⓒ Type these bulleted paragraphs, tapping Enter after each.

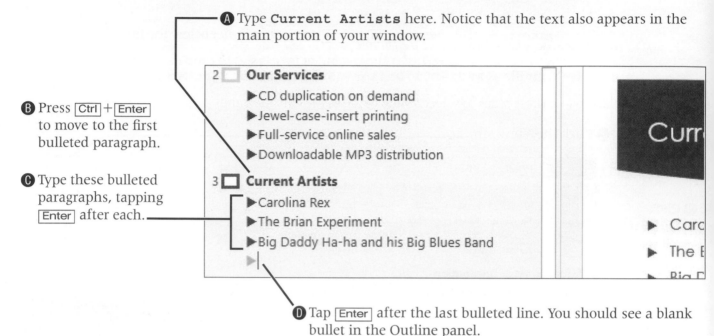

2 ☐ **Our Services**
  ▶CD duplication on demand
  ▶Jewel-case-insert printing
  ▶Full-service online sales
  ▶Downloadable MP3 distribution

3 ☐ **Current Artists**
  ▶Carolina Rex
  ▶The Brian Experiment
  ▶Big Daddy Ha-ha and his Big Blues Band
  ▶

Ⓓ Tap Enter after the last bulleted line. You should see a blank bullet in the Outline panel.

PowerPoint adds a new slide to the presentation whenever the insertion point is positioned within the last box on a slide and the Ctrl + Enter *keystroke combination is issued. At this point, you should have a new, bulleted paragraph visible in the outline below the* Big Daddy Ha-ha *paragraph.*

6. Follow these steps to promote a paragraph to make a new slide:

Ⓐ Ensure that the insertion point is on the blank bulleted paragraph in the outline.

Ⓑ Choose **Home→Paragraph→ Decrease List Level** 🔽.

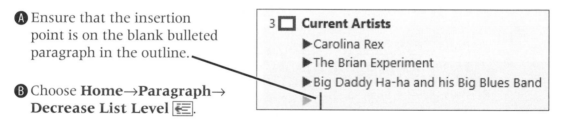

3 ☐ **Current Artists**
  ▶Carolina Rex
  ▶The Brian Experiment
  ▶Big Daddy Ha-ha and his Big Blues Band
  ▶

PowerPoint promotes the bulleted paragraph to create a new slide.

7. Type **New Artist Specials** and tap Enter.

Tapping Enter *created a new slide. You must use* Ctrl + Enter *to add a bulleted paragraph after a slide's title. However, you will fix this by demoting the new slide in the next step.*

8. Choose **Home→Paragraph→Increase List Level** 🔼.

The new slide created when you tapped Enter *in step 7 has been converted to a bullet under the New Artist Specials title.*

9. Complete the new slide in the outline as shown, tapping Enter after each paragraph (including the last one).

Bulleted Paragraphs	▪ 25% discount on CD duplication [Enter]
	▪ Five free T-shirts [Enter]
	▪ 10% discount on promotional items [Enter]
	▪ Valid until July 20 [Enter]

10. Choose **Home→Paragraph→Decrease List Level** ⇤ to promote the new paragraph that follows the *Valid until July 20* paragraph and convert it into a new slide.

11. Type **Contact Us** and then use ⌐Ctrl⌐+⌐Enter⌐ to create a bullet below the title.

12. Taking care not to tap ⌐Enter⌐ after the last bullet in this slide, complete the new slide as shown.

Bulleted Paragraphs
- Call
- (800) 555-1212
- Or
- Email us at
- iJams@example.com

13. Save your presentation.

Collapsing and Expanding Slides

Video Library   http://labyrinthelab.com/videos   Video Number: PP13-V0203

As the Outline panel grows, it can be difficult to manage your slides when all the bulleted text is showing. PowerPoint lets you collapse slides so that only the title is visible. This makes it easier to manage your slides because more slides will be visible in the Outline panel.

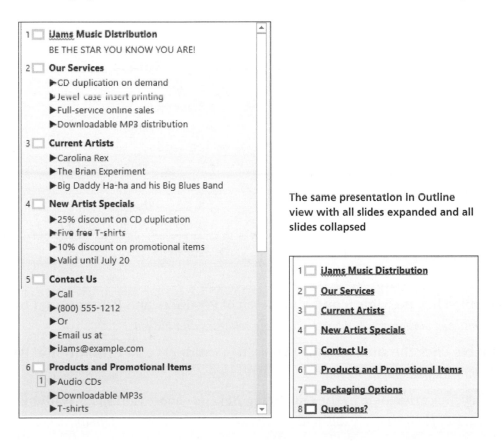

The same presentation in Outline view with all slides expanded and all slides collapsed

Use the Context Menu on the Outline Panel

In this exercise, you will use the context menu from the Outline panel.

1. Save your file as **PP02-D03-Design-[FirstInitialLastName]**.

2. Follow these steps to explore the Outline panel:

Ⓐ Scroll until **Products and Promotional Items** and **Packaging Options** are visible.

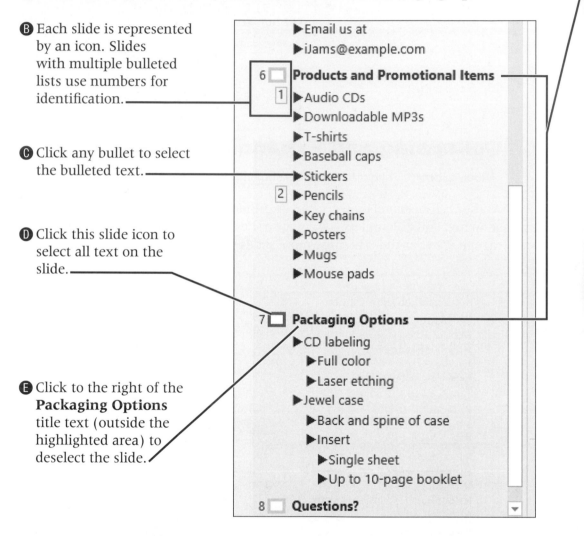

Ⓑ Each slide is represented by an icon. Slides with multiple bulleted lists use numbers for identification.

Ⓒ Click any bullet to select the bulleted text.

Ⓓ Click this slide icon to select all text on the slide.

Ⓔ Click to the right of the **Packaging Options** title text (outside the highlighted area) to deselect the slide.

3. Double-click the **slide icon** ☐ to the left of **Products and Promotional Items**.
The bulleted paragraphs beneath the title are collapsed and hidden.

4. Double-click the **slide icon** ☐ to the left of **Products and Promotional Items** again.
The bulleted paragraphs beneath the title are expanded and are once again visible.

5. Right-click anywhere in the **Outline panel** and choose **Collapse→Collapse All**.
All bulleted paragraphs are collapsed and hidden. Only the slide titles remain visible.

6. Right-click anywhere in the **Outline panel** and choose **Expand→Expand All**.
All bulleted paragraphs are expanded and are once again visible.

Move a Slide

The easiest way to move a slide in an outline is to first collapse all slides. Then you can click the desired slide title and drag it to its new position.

7. Right-click anywhere in the **Outline panel** and choose **Collapse→Collapse All**.

8. If necessary, scroll up until all slide icons and titles are visible in the **Outline panel**.

9. Follow these steps to move a slide:

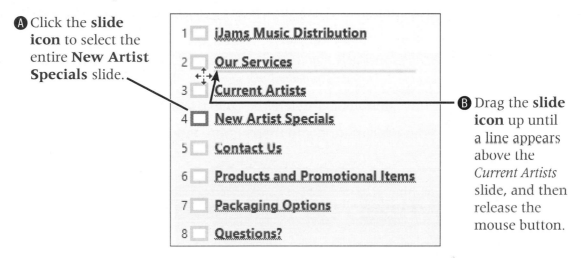

Ⓐ Click the **slide icon** to select the entire **New Artist Specials** slide.

Ⓑ Drag the **slide icon** up until a line appears above the *Current Artists* slide, and then release the mouse button.

The New Artists Specials slide appears above the Current Artists slide.

10. Using this same method, move the **Packaging Options** slide to the second position, just below the title slide.

11. Save your presentation.

Deleting Slides

Video Library   http://labyrinthelab.com/videos   Video Number: PP13-V0204

You can delete a slide from a presentation by clicking the slide icon in the Outline panel to select the entire slide and then tapping the ⌊Delete⌋ key. Likewise, slides can be deleted in Normal and Slide Sorter views by choosing the desired slide(s) and tapping ⌊Delete⌋. If you inadvertently delete a slide, you can use the Undo button on the Quick Access toolbar to undo the latest action and restore the deleted slide. If you later decide that you want to keep the change, click the Redo button on the Quick Access toolbar to go back to the previous action.

FROM THE KEYBOARD
⌊Delete⌋ to remove a slide

PowerPoint 2013

Delete a Slide from the Outline

In this exercise, you will delete slides using the Outline panel.

1. Save your file as **PP02-D04-Design-[FirstInitialLastName]**.

2. Right-click anywhere in the **Outline panel** and choose **Expand→Expand All**.

3. Click the **Current Artists slide icon** ☐ (not the title text) to select the entire slide.

4. Tap Delete to remove the slide.

   A faded bullet may appear at the end of the previous slide. This is PowerPoint readying itself for additional text. The ghost bullet will not display on the slide itself.

5. Using this same method, delete the **Questions** slide.

6. Save your presentation and then choose **File→Close** to close it.

Working with Word Integration

Video Library   http://labyrinthelab.com/videos   Video Number: PP13-V0205

Microsoft Word is an excellent word processing program that integrates with PowerPoint. Outlines created in Word can easily be converted to a PowerPoint presentation. You may need to create a presentation based on an outline someone else created in Word, or you may find it easier to plan a presentation using a Word outline rather than starting PowerPoint first and wondering what slides you will create.

Creating a Presentation Outline in Word

Word's powerful outlining tool makes setting up and modifying outlines easy. You can create an outline in Word and import it to PowerPoint. To use Word outlines in PowerPoint, you must apply the appropriate styles to the paragraphs in the Word document prior to importing the outline. PowerPoint converts the Word outline by using these rules:

- All level-1 paragraphs translate to Titles in a PowerPoint slide.
- All level-2 paragraphs translate to level-1 body bullets in a PowerPoint slide.
- All level-3 paragraphs translate to level-2 body bullets in a PowerPoint slide.

Once a Word outline is imported into PowerPoint, you can promote or demote the bullets, apply layouts and a design theme, and make other enhancements.

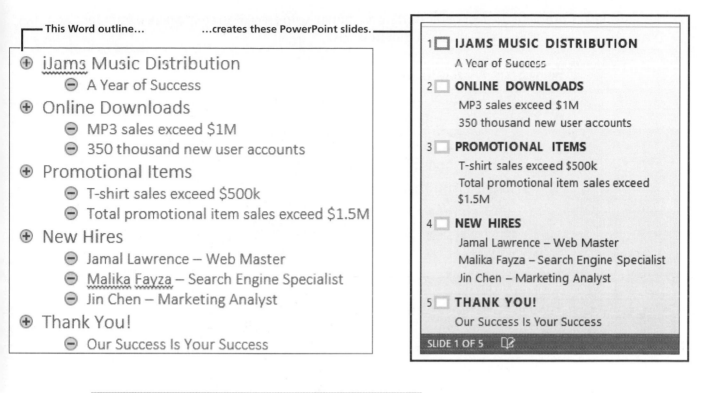

This Word outline...   ...creates these PowerPoint slides.

Create a Presentation and Import a Word Outline

In this exercise, you will create an outline in Word, use it to generate slides for a new presentation, and then modify the presentation.

1. Start **Word** and create a new, blank document.

2. Save your file as **PP02-D05-WordOutline-[FirstInitialLastName]** to the **PP2013 Lesson 02** folder.

   In the next few steps, you will type and apply Word styles to paragraphs.

3. With the blank document open, choose **View→Views→Outline**.

4. Type **iJams Music Distribution** and tap Enter.

5. Tap Tab. Then type **A Year of Success** and tap Enter.

   Tapping Tab increases the list level and creates a level-2 style.

6. Press Shift+Tab. Then type **Online Downloads** and tap Enter.

   Pressing Shift+Tab decreases the list level and returns the text to a level-1 style.

   Next, you will create two level-2-styled paragraphs that will eventually be converted to text bullets in a PowerPoint slide.

7. Tap Tab. Then type **MP3 sales exceed $1M** and tap Enter.

8. Type **350 thousand new user accounts** and tap Enter.

9. Now press Shift+Tab to return the indentation level to a level-1 style.

   You are now ready to continue typing the rest of the outline.

10. Complete the rest of the outline as shown, using [Enter] to create new paragraphs and [Tab] and [Shift]+[Tab] to adjust indent levels.

11. Save the file. Then close the outline and Word.

Word closes, and PowerPoint is visible.

Import the Outline

12. If necessary, restore **PowerPoint** from the **taskbar** (or start it, if necessary).

13. Choose **File→New** and click the **Blank Presentation** icon.

14. Save your file as `PP02-D05-WordOutline-[FirstInitialLastName]` to the **PP2013 Lesson 02** folder.

You can use the same filename as the Word document because the Word and PowerPoint files have different file extensions.

15. Choose **Design→Themes→More** [▼]**→Ion** to apply a document theme.

16. Locate the **Design→Variants** group on the Ribbon and click the **third variation** (the purple one) to apply it to all slides.

17. Choose **Home→Slides→New Slide menu** ▼**→Slides From Outline**.

18. Use the **Insert Outline** dialog box to navigate to the **PP2013 Lesson 02** folder.

19. Choose **PP02-D05-WordOutline-[FirstInitialLastName]** and click **Insert**.

PowerPoint will take a moment to import the outline. Note that the first slide is blank because PowerPoint inserted the slides from the outline after the existing blank title slide.

20. Choose **View→Presentation Views→Outline View** and examine the PowerPoint outline.

Each level-1 paragraph from the outline has become a slide title, and each level-2 paragraph has become a bulleted paragraph under the appropriate title.

21. Choose **View→Presentation Views→Normal** to view the slide thumbnails.

22. Choose the first slide (the blank one) and tap ⌨Delete⌨.

    The blank slide is deleted, and the iJams Music Distribution slide becomes selected.

Change a Layout

23. Choose **Home→Slides→Layout menu ▼→Title Slide**.

    The layout of the selected slide changes.

24. Select the final slide, **Thank You**, and choose **Home→Slides→ Layout menu ▼→ Section Header**.

25. Choose the first slide, **iJams Music Distribution**.

    Each slide is formatted with blue text because Word formatted the heading styles as blue.

Reset the Slide Formatting

26. With the first slide selected, choose **Home→Slides→Reset**.

    The text formatting is removed and returns to the default setting for the current document theme. The slide subtitle is converted to uppercase because that is the formatting of the Ion theme.

27. Select the second slide, press ⌨Shift⌨, select the last slide, and release ⌨Shift⌨.

    Slides 2–5 become selected.

28. Choose **Home→Slides→Reset** to reformat the text on the selected slides with the document theme formatting.

29. Save your presentation.

Formatting Your Presentation

Video Library   http://labyrinthelab.com/videos   Video Number: PP13-V0206

PowerPoint 2013 makes it so easy to create a presentation that the slides you create may not need any additional formatting. After all, the placeholders arrange the text, the bullets are automatic, and the color scheme is preformatted. However, in most cases, you will want to fine-tune your presentation. Formatting your presentation will make a good presentation even better.

Formatting Text

Formatting text is a common step in presentation development. For instance, when reviewing a slide, you might decide that the text could be emphasized by changing the font color. If you had the time, you could change the font color of each piece of text on the slide individually by using the Font group on the Home tab of the Ribbon. However, a more efficient way to change the font color is to first select the placeholder and then apply the color change. By selecting the placeholder, all text within the placeholder is changed in one swoop. The following illustration describes the buttons on the Home tab's Font group that assist you in formatting text.

FROM THE RIBBON

Home→Font→Bold

Home→Font→Underline

Home→Font→Italic

FROM THE KEYBOARD

Ctrl+B for bold

Ctrl+U for underline

Ctrl+I for italic

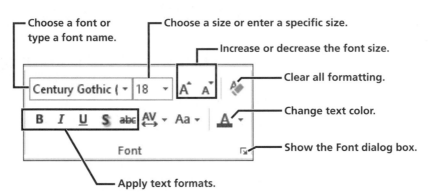

- Choose a font or type a font name.
- Choose a size or enter a specific size.
- Increase or decrease the font size.
- Clear all formatting.
- Change text color.
- Show the Font dialog box.
- Apply text formats.

Setting Character Spacing

Character spacing refers to the horizontal space between characters. PowerPoint lets you adjust this spacing to give your text some breathing room. If none of the preset options fit your needs, you can enter a numerical value to specify the exact amount of spacing. In the professional world of print, this is referred to as *tracking* or *kerning*. You must first select characters before applying character spacing, or select the placeholder to apply spacing to all the text.

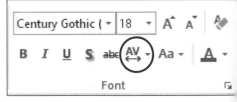

- MP3 sales exceed $1M
- 350 thousand new user accounts

- M P 3   s a l e s   e x c e e d $ 1 M
- 3 5 0   t h o u s a n d   n e w   u s e r   a c c o u n t s

The same slide with no character spacing (left) and a large amount of character spacing applied (right)

Setting the Text Case

A quick way to populate your slides with text is to copy text from an existing source, such as from an email message or Word document. However, the original text may not be formatted in the case appropriate for your slide. You can easily change the case of text, saving you from having to retype it.

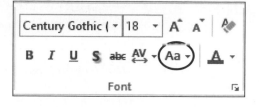

The following table illustrates the options available with the Change Case button.

TEXT CASE OPTIONS	
Menu Option	**How It Affects Text**
Sentence Case	Your text will look like this.
Lowercase	your text will look like this.
Uppercase	YOUR TEXT WILL LOOK LIKE THIS.
Capitalize Each Word	Your Text Will Look Like This.
Toggle Case	Wherever you typed an uppercase letter, it will become lowercase. Wherever you typed a lowercase letter, it will become uppercase.
	Example: If you type Your Text Will Look Like This, Toggle Case will change it to yOUR tEXT wILL lOOK lIKE tHIS.

Format Text

In this exercise, you will change the formatting of the fonts in the Title and Subtitle.

1. Save your file as **PP02-D06-WordOutline-[FirstInitialLastName]**.

2. Choose **View→Presentation Views→Normal** to return to Normal view, if necessary.

3. Display the **Home** tab so you can see the font settings as you work.

4. Click the title slide (the first one) to select it.

5. Follow these steps to select the subtitle placeholder box:

Ⓐ Click anywhere on the text to position the insertion point inside the handles for this text box. The dashed line indicates the text box border.

Ⓑ Click any edge of the dashed border to change it to a solid border (shown here).

The solid line indicates that the text box is selected. Any formatting change you make now will affect all text within the box. Notice also that the Font Size box on the Ribbon is currently set to 20. The Ion theme applied this font size to the subtitle.

6. Choose **Home→Font→Increase Font Size** Ａ to increase the font size to **24**.

7. Choose **Home→Font→Bold** ⓑ.

PowerPoint makes the text bold.

8. Choose **Home→Font→Shadow** ⓢ.

The text stands out from the page a bit more because there is now a slight drop-shadow effect.

Format the Title

9. Click on the text of the title, **iJams Music Distribution**, and then click once on the dashed-line border to select the Title text box.

10. Choose **Home→Font→Font Size** ▼ and point to several different font sizes.

Notice how Live Preview displays the slide title size changes as you point to different settings on the Font Size menu.

11. Set the **font size** to **96**.

The text is not large enough. There is still some room to enlarge it so that the company name dominates the slide.

12. Click **96** in the **Home→Font→Font Size** menu.

13. Type **115** and tap ⌷Enter⌷.

PowerPoint increases the size of the text to 115. You can select a font size from the menu or type in your own value.

14. Save the presentation.

Setting Line Spacing

Video Library   http://labyrinthelab.com/videos   Video Number: PP13-V0207

Sometimes, instead of changing the font size or adding many hard returns, you need to only increase or decrease the spacing between lines to have the proper effect. Line spacing determines the amount of space between lines of text.

This setting is useful if text appears cramped and you wish to open up some breathing room between lines.

The same slide before and after applying Line Spacing

Adjust the Line Spacing

In this exercise, you will adjust the line spacing to increase the amount of space between bullets.

1. Save your file as **PP02-D07-WordOutline-[FirstInitialLastName]**.

2. Display the **New Hires** slide.

3. Click any of the names to display a dashed border.

4. Click the dashed border to select the entire text box.

5. Choose **Home→Paragraph→Line Spacing** ⇕≡→**2.0** to increase the spacing.
   PowerPoint redistributes the bulleted text vertically on the slide with more spacing between items.

6. Save and close your presentation.

Setting Paragraph Alignment

Video Library   http://labyrinthelab.com/videos   Video Number: PP13-V0208

In time, you will be able to "eye" a presentation and notice if the paragraph alignment is not balanced. You can select one or more paragraphs and then click an alignment button on the Ribbon to make the change. Use the following buttons from the Home→Paragraph group on the Ribbon to realign paragraphs.

PARAGRAPH ALIGNMENT BUTTONS		
Purpose	**Button**	**Example**
Left-align	▤	This text has been left aligned. Notice how the left edge is in a straight line, but the right edge appears jagged.
Center-align	▤	This text has been center aligned. Notice how the text is balanced and centered.
Right-align	▤	This text has been right aligned. Notice how the right edge is in a straight line.
Justify	▤	This text has been justify aligned. Notice how the text is spaced to maintain straight lines on the left and right.

It is often easiest to read left-aligned text because the eye can more easily find the starting point of subsequent lines.

PowerPoint 2013

Format the Contact Us Slide

In this exercise, you will reformat the Contact Us slide.

1. Open **PP02-D08-Contact** from your **PP2013 Lesson 02** folder and save it as **PP02-D08-Contact-[FirstInitialLastName]**.

2. If necessary, scroll down; select **slide 5, Contact Us**.

3. Click in the bulleted list and then click a border of the text box.

4. Choose **Home→Paragraph→Bullets** to remove the bullets.

5. Choose **Home→Paragraph→Center**.

6. Select the entire telephone number.

   A faded formatting box appears. Pointing your mouse at it will cause it to become more visible. You may format the selected text from this formatting box, but we will use the Ribbon as in the next steps.

7. Choose **Home→Font→Font Size** ▼ and increase the size to **32**.

8. Using the same method, increase the size of the last line (the email address) to **32**.

9. Save your presentation.

Using the Format Painter

Video Library   http://labyrinthelab.com/videos   Video Number: PP13-V0209

Common to all Office programs, the Format Painter is a great tool that simplifies the formatting process. The Format Painter copies all text formats including the typeface, size, color, and attributes such as bold, italic, and underline. It also copies formatting applied to shapes or clip art. The Format Painter helps you easily maintain a standardized, uniform look in your presentation.

Loading the Format Painter

The key to using the Format Painter successfully is understanding when it is loaded. After formatting has been copied to the Format Painter, its Ribbon icon appears pressed in. This pressed-in icon indicates that the Format Painter is loaded and ready to use.

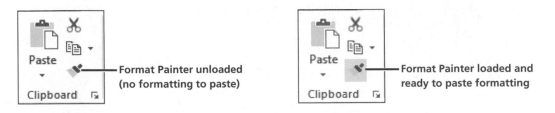

Format Painter unloaded (no formatting to paste)   Format Painter loaded and ready to paste formatting

QUICK REFERENCE	COPYING FORMATS WITH THE FORMAT PAINTER
Task	**Procedure**
Copy formats with the Format Painter	■ Select the object (text, picture, drawn line, etc.) with the format you wish to copy. ■ Choose Home→Clipboard→Format Painter 🖌. ■ Select the object at the new location to which you wish to copy formatting.
Use the Format Painter repeatedly	■ Select the object with formatting to be copied. ■ Double-click Home→Clipboard→Format Painter 🖌. ■ Click with the Format Painter on all objects to which you wish the formatting copied. (The Format Painter will remain active until you switch it off.) ■ Click once on the Format Painter to switch it off again, or tap Esc.

TIP

When the Format Painter is loaded, the mouse pointer changes from an arrow 🔍 to a brush 🖌.

DEVELOP YOUR SKILLS PP02-D09

Copy Formatting with the Format Painter

In this exercise, you will copy and paste text formatting with the Format Painter.

1. Save your file as **PP02-D09-Contact-[FirstInitialLastName]**.

2. Select the fourth slide, **New Artist Specials**.

3. Double-click *free* in the second bullet to select it.

4. Choose **Home→Font→Font Size→32**.

5. Choose **Home→Font→Text Shadow S**.

6. Follow these steps to choose a font color:

   Ⓐ Choose **Home→Font→Font Color menu ▼**.   Ⓑ Locate the **Theme Colors**.

   Ⓒ Click the eighth color, **Orange, Accent 4**.

7. Choose **Home→Clipboard→Format Painter 🖌**.

   The Format Painter icon is pressed in and is now loaded.

8. Click once on *July* in the last bullet.

   The formatting is copied to the word July, *and the Format Painter icon on the Ribbon becomes unloaded.*

9. Choose **Home→Clipboard→Format Painter** ✏️.

   The Format Painter has been reloaded with the formatting from the word July because that is where the insertion point is.

10. Click once on *20* in the last bullet.

    The formatting is copied to 20, and the Format Painter on the Ribbon becomes unloaded.

Use the Format Painter Repeatedly

11. Select the third slide, **Our Services**.

12. Drag across *on demand* in the first bullet to select it.

13. Choose **Home→Font→Bold** B.

14. Choose **Home→Font→Italic** I.

15. Choose **Home→Font→Font Color** ▼**→Theme Colors→Red Accent 2**.

16. Double-click **Home→Clipboard→Format Painter** ✏️.

    Double-clicking the Format Painter will keep it loaded until you turn it off.

17. Click the word *online* in the third bullet.

    The formatting is copied to online, *and the Format Painter remains loaded.*

18. Click the word *sales* in the third bullet.

19. Click the words *MP3* and *distribution* in the last bullet.

20. Choose **Home→Clipboard→Format Painter** ✏️.

    The Format Painter has been unloaded.

21. Save your presentation.

Using the Slide Sorter

Video Library   http://labyrinthelab.com/videos   Video Number: PP13-V0210

Up until now, you've been working in Normal view, which is good for manipulating a handful of slides. However, as your presentation grows to more slides than are visible in Normal view, you will want to explore the function of Slide Sorter view.

Rearranging Slides

PowerPoint's Slide Sorter view is used to rearrange slides. In Slide Sorter view, each slide is a thumbnail image so the entire presentation is visible at a glance. As your presentation grows, often the order of the slides needs to be changed to create a logical concept flow. Using the Drag and Drop method in Slide Sorter view, you can quickly reorganize your slides by moving them to the correct spot.

Use the Slide Sorter View

In this exercise, you will practice using Slide Sorter view.

1. Save your file as **PP02-D10-Contact-[FirstInitialLastName]**.

2. Choose **View→Presentation Views→Slide Sorter** ⊞ .

3. Follow these steps to move a slide:

Ⓐ If necessary, drag the **Zoom** slider to change the zoom percentage until all six slides are shown. (Your slides may display differently.)

Ⓑ Drag the **Our Services** slide to the left of **Packaging Options**. (Your slides may display differently.)

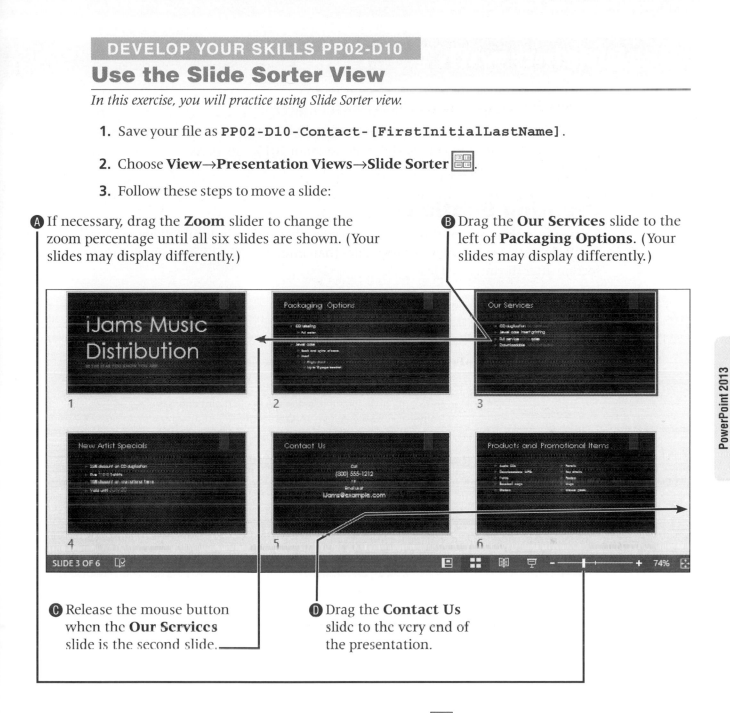

Ⓒ Release the mouse button when the **Our Services** slide is the second slide.

Ⓓ Drag the **Contact Us** slide to the very end of the presentation.

4. Choose **Views→Presentation Views→Normal** ⊟ .

5. Save and close the presentation.

PowerPoint 2013

Organizing with Sections

Video Library   http://labyrinthelab.com/videos   Video Number: PP13-V0211

Using the Slide Sorter with individual slides works well for small presentations. For presentations containing many slides, PowerPoint 2013's Sections feature helps you keep them organized.

Creating Sections

Sections are always created before the selected slide and include all following slides. This often results in a section containing more slides than intended. The fix is to simply create another section after the intended last slide.

QUICK REFERENCE	USING SECTIONS
Task	**Procedure**
Create a section	▪ Select the first slide from the Slides panel for the section. ▪ Choose Home→Slides→Section→Add Section. ▪ Select the slide after the last in the section and choose Home→Slides→Section→Add Section.
Name a section	▪ Right-click the section's title bar and choose Rename Section. ▪ Type the new name for the section and click Rename.
Move a section	▪ Drag a section's title bar above/below another section title bar.
Collapse or expand a section	▪ Double-click the section's title bar.
Remove a section	▪ Right-click the section's title bar and choose Remove Section (delete section and leave slides); choose Remove Section & Slides (delete section and its slides).

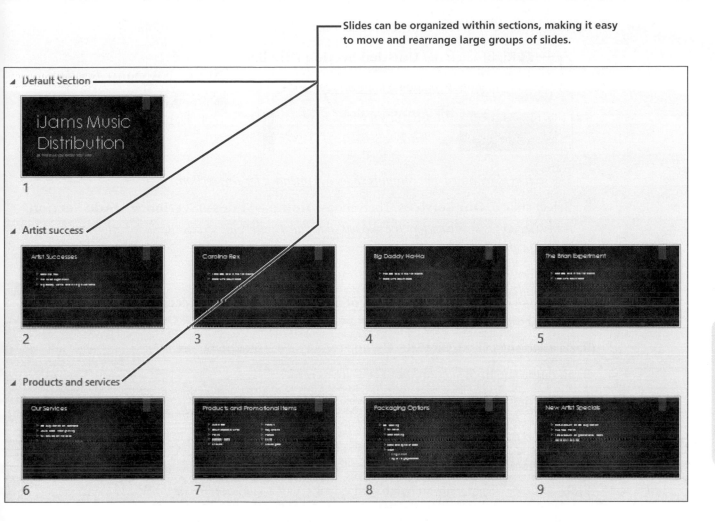

Slides can be organized within sections, making it easy to move and rearrange large groups of slides.

Create Sections

In this exercise, you will create sections.

1. Open **PP02-D11-Sections** from your **PP2013 Lesson 02** folder and save it as **PP02-D11-Sections-[FirstInitialLastName]**.

   With so many slides, it may be easier to work in Slide Sorter view.

2. Choose **View→Presentation Views→Slide Sorter**.

3. Select slide 2, **Artist Successes**. Then choose **Home→Slides→Section ▼→Add Section**.

   A new section named Untitled Section is created before the selected slide. Every slide below it is included in the section.

4. Follow these steps to rename the section:

Ⓐ Right-click the **Untitled Section title bar**.

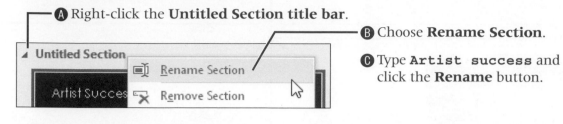

Ⓑ Choose **Rename Section**.

Ⓒ Type **Artist success** and click the **Rename** button.

The section is renamed, but contains slides not intended for this section.

5. Select slide 6, **Our Services**. Then choose **Home→Slides→Section ▼→Add Section**.
A new section is started before the selected slide, but PowerPoint scrolls the Slide Sorter window to the top of the presentation.

6. Scroll down until you see the new, untitled section.

7. Right-click the **Untitled Section** title bar, choose **Rename Section**, and rename the section to **Products and services**.

8. Click the last slide, **Contact Us**, and create a new section before it.

9. Rename the final section **Call to action**.

10. Save your presentation.

Managing Sections

Video Library   http://labyrinthelab.com/videos   Video Number: PP13-V0212

Once sections have been created, they can be dragged and rearranged in either the Slides panel or Slide Sorter view. Individual slides can even be dragged from one section to another. Additionally, sections can be collapsed, similar to slide titles in Outline view. Collapsed sections hide the slides, making it easy to drag and reorder the sections. However, the collapsed sections hide slides only when editing. The collapsed slides will display as normal when running the slide show.

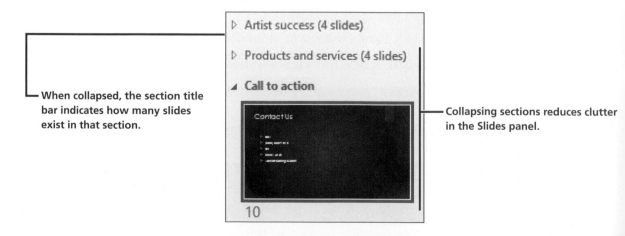

When collapsed, the section title bar indicates how many slides exist in that section.

Collapsing sections reduces clutter in the Slides panel.

Manage Sections

In this exercise, you will rearrange slides by using sections.

1. Save your presentation as **PP02-D12-Sections-[FirstInitialLastName]**.

2. With the presentation still displaying Slide Sorter view, scroll until you can see the **Artist success** section title bar, if necessary.

3. Double-click the **Artist success** section title bar to collapse it.

4. Double-click the **Products and services** section title bar.

5. Choose **View→Presentation Views→Normal**.

   The sections do not remain collapsed when you change views.

6. Follow these steps to rearrange the sections:

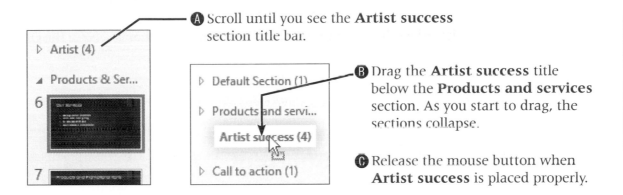

Ⓐ Scroll until you see the **Artist success** section title bar.

Ⓑ Drag the **Artist success** title below the **Products and services** section. As you start to drag, the sections collapse.

Ⓒ Release the mouse button when **Artist success** is placed properly.

7. Choose **View→Presentation Views→Slide Sorter**.

8. Click anywhere in the gray area outside the slide thumbnails to deselect any slides.

9. Scroll down, if necessary, until you see the entire **Call to Action** section with the **Contact Us** slide.

10. Use the **Zoom slider**, if necessary, to make the view smaller.

    You should see all slides in both the Products and Services and Call to Action sections.

11. Drag the last slide of the **Products and Services** section (New Artist Specials) to the left of the **Contact Us** slide to move it to the Call to Action section.

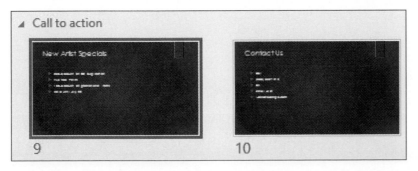

12. Save your presentation.

PowerPoint 2013

Printing Your Presentation

Video Library   http://labyrinthelab.com/videos   Video Number: PP13-V0213

Ninety percent of the time, you will be viewing or projecting the presentations you create from a PC or notebook computer. However, there may be times when a hard copy of the presentation is needed. In this lesson, you will simply explore the options of printing a presentation.

Knowing What You Can Print

PowerPoint can create the following types of printouts:

- **Slides:** Prints each slide of a presentation on a separate page
- **Handouts:** Prints one or more slides per page, leaving room for attendees to jot notes during the presentation
- **Speaker Notes:** Prints each slide on a separate page, with any speaker notes you created for the slide below
- **Outline:** Prints a text outline of each slide, similar to what is seen in the Outline panel

Previewing a Printout

The Print window, found in Backstage view, lets you see how each slide will be printed. You can then refine the appearance before printing.

FROM THE RIBBON
File→Print to display the Print tab in Backstage view

Using the Print Shortcut

If you have customized your Quick Access toolbar to display the Quick Print icon, you may find it tempting to just click it. However, before this becomes a habit, know that a click of this button sends the entire presentation to the current printer, whether or not you want to make adjustments. If you are working with a document theme that has a colored background, the printing process will not only be painstakingly slow, but may also waste your toner or ink!

FROM THE KEYBOARD
Ctrl+P to display the Print tab in Backstage view

The Quick Print button on the Quick Access toolbar sends your presentation directly to the printer.

Preview a Printout

In this exercise, you will use Backstage view to preview a printout.

1. Choose **File→Print**.
2. Follow these steps to examine the print options:

Ⓐ Use the **left arrow** or scroll bar to return to the first slide.

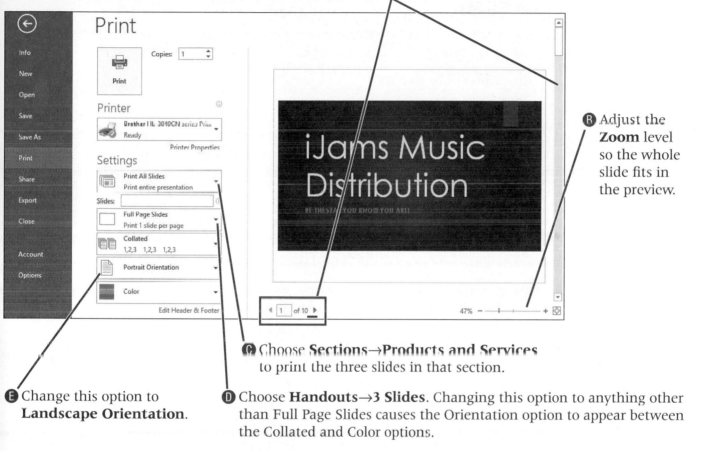

Ⓑ Adjust the **Zoom** level so the whole slide fits in the preview.

Ⓒ Choose **Sections→Products and Services** to print the three slides in that section.

Ⓔ Change this option to **Landscape Orientation**.

Ⓓ Choose **Handouts→3 Slides**. Changing this option to anything other than Full Page Slides causes the Orientation option to appear between the Collated and Color options.

3. Click the **Back** ⓔ button at the top of Backstage view to return to the main PowerPoint screen without printing. Close **PowerPoint**.

Concepts Review

To check your knowledge of the key concepts introduced in this lesson, complete the Concepts Review quiz by choosing the appropriate access option below.

If you are...	Then access the quiz by...
Using the Labyrinth Video Library	Going to http://labyrinthelab.com/videos
Using eLab	Logging in, choosing Content, and navigating to the Concepts Review quiz for this lesson
Not using the Labyrinth Video Library or eLab	Going to the student resource center for this book

PowerPoint 2013

Reinforce Your Skills

Work with Outlines and Formatting

In this exercise, you will format some slides in the Kids for Change presentation.

Work with Slides

1. Start **PowerPoint**. Open **PP02-R01-Design** from the **PP2013 Lesson 02** folder and save it as `PP02-R01-Design-[FirstInitialLastName]`.

2. Select the second slide, **Events**.

3. Choose **Home→Slides→Layout→Two Content** to change the slide layout to a two-column layout.

4. Select the last four paragraphs in the left column and drag them to the right column.

Work with Outlines

5. Choose **View→Presentation Views→Outline View**.

6. Locate the **Program Benefits** slide in the Outline panel.

7. Click to the right of the word *health* in the last paragraph of the **Program Benefits** slide in the Outline panel.

8. Tap Ctrl + Enter to create a slide.

9. Type `Requirements` in the Outline panel as the slide title.

10. Tap Enter and then tap Tab to create a new, bulleted paragraph.

11. Type `You need` in the Outline panel.

12. Tap Enter and then tap Tab to create a new, bulleted paragraph.

13. Type `Positive attitude`, tap Enter, and type `Strong work ethic` to create another indented paragraph.

14. Tap Enter and then tap Shift + Tab to create and demote the next bullet.

15. Type `Time commitment`.

16. Tap Enter and then tap Tab.

17. Type `One monthly event`, tap Enter, and type `One annual meeting` to create the final two paragraphs.

18. Choose **Home→Slides→Layout→Title and Content**.

Format a Presentation

19. Choose **View→Presentation Views→Normal** and select the title slide from the **Slides** panel.

20. Click the **Title** box, and then click again on the edge of the box to select it.

21. Choose **Home→Font→Increase Font Size** once to increase the font size to **60**.

22. Choose **Home→Font→Bold**.

23. Display the **Requirements** slide on the Slides panel.

24. Choose **Home→Slides→New Slide**.

25. Type **Remember** as the title.

26. Type the following as bulleted paragraphs:
    - `Think globally, act locally.`
    - `Or think locally, act globally.`
    - `Just...`
    - `Think and act!`

27. Select the bulleted text box by clicking the border.

28. Choose **Home→Paragraph→Bullets** to remove the bullets from all paragraphs.

29. Choose **Home→Paragraph→Center** to center the text on the slide.

30. Choose **Home→Paragraph→Line Spacing→2.0** to increase the vertical spacing between bullets.

31. Select the text *think and act!*

32. Choose **Home→Font→Increase Font Size** four times to increase the size to 32.

Use Format Painter

33. With the *think and act!* text still selected, double-click the **Home→Clipboard→Format Painter** button to load it for multiple uses.

34. Click the words *Think* and *act* in the first line, and then click the words *think* and *act* in the second line to duplicate the formatting.

35. Choose **Home→Clipboard→Format Painter** to turn off the Format Painter.

36. Save the presentation; submit your final file based on the guidelines provided by your instructor. Exit **PowerPoint**.

    To view examples of how your file or files should look at the end of this exercise, go to the student resource center.

Import from Word; Organize and Print a Presentation

In this exercise, you will import an outline from Word, create sections, rearrange sections and slides, and print a slide.

Integrate with Word

1. Start **Microsoft Word**. Open **PP02-R02-Outline** from the **PP2013 Lesson 02** folder.

2. Choose **View→Views→Outline**.

3. Read over the outline. Then close **Word**.

4. Start **PowerPoint** and click **Blank Presentation**.

5. Save your file as **PP02-R02-Outline-[FirstInitialLastName]** in the **PP2013 Lesson 02** folder.

6. Choose **Design→Themes→Ion** to apply a design theme.

7. Choose **Home→Slides→New Slide ▼→Slides from Outline** to begin importing the Word outline.

8. Navigate to your **PP2013 Lesson 02** folder and double-click the **PP02-R02-Outline** Word document to import the outline and create the slides.

9. Select **slide 1** in the Slides panel and tap Delete to delete the blank slide.

10. Click **slide 1** in the Slides panel to ensure it is selected, scroll to the bottom of the Slides panel, and Shift +click the final slide, **slide 7**, so all slides are selected.

11. Choose **Home→Slides→Reset** to reset the formatting of all slides.

Organize with Sections

12. Click slide 2, **College Application**, in the Slides panel to select it and deselect the others.

13. Choose **Home→Slides→Section→Add Section** to add a new section starting with the **College Application** slide.

14. Choose **Home→Slides→Section→Rename Section**.

15. Type **Personal Benefits** and then click **Rename**.

16. Click slide 4, **Crime Reduction**, in the Slides panel to select it and deselect the others.

17. Choose **Home→Slides→Section→Add Section** to add a new section starting with the **College Application** slide.

18. Choose **Home→Slides→Section→Rename Section**.

19. Type **Community Benefits** and then click **Rename**.

Use the Slide Sorter

20. Choose **View→Presentation Views→Slide Sorter**.

21. Drag the **Zoom** slider in the lower-right area of the PowerPoint window until all seven slides are visible.

22. Drag the **Leadership Skills** slide so it is between the College Application and Sense of Accomplishment slides.

23. Drag the **Community Benefits** section header up so that it is before the Personal Benefits section.

24. Save the presentation.

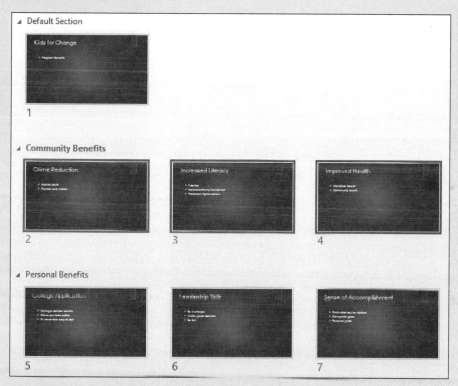

Print Your Presentation

25. Choose **File→Print** to display the Print tab in Backstage view.

26. Use the scroll bar at the right of the PowerPoint window to navigate the slides until slide 3, **Increased Literacy**, displays.

27. Choose your printer from the **Printer** option. Your instructor may prefer you to choose the PDF option.

28. Opt to print only the current slide; opt to print full-page slides, one slide per page.

29. Set the color option to **Grayscale**; print one copy.

30. Submit your final file based on guidelines provided by your instructor. Exit **PowerPoint**.

    To view examples of how your file or files should look at the end of this exercise, go to the student resource center.

Create a Presentation from a Word Outline

In this exercise, you will import a Word outline to create the initial slides. You will then reset the formatting of the slides and arrange the slides into sections. Finally, you will print a slide.

Import an Outline and Reset Formatting

1. Start **PowerPoint** and click **Blank Presentation**.

2. Save your file as **PP02-R03-Outline-[FirstInitialLastName]** in the **PP2013 Lesson 02** folder.

3. Choose **Design→Themes→Retrospect** to apply a design theme.

4. Choose **Home→Slides→New Slide ▼→Slides from Outline** to begin importing a Word outline.

5. Navigate to your **PP2013 Lesson 02** folder and double-click the **PPT02-R03-Outline** Word document to import the outline and create the slides.

6. Select **slide 1** in the Slides panel and tap [Delete] to delete the blank slide.

7. Click **slide 1** in the Slides panel to ensure it is selected, scroll to the bottom of the Slides panel, and [Shift]+click the final slide, **slide 6**, so that all slides are selected.

8. Choose **Home→Slides→Reset** to reset the formatting of all slides.

Create Additional Slides

9. Choose **Views→Presentation Views→Outline View**.

10. Locate the **Bully No More** slide in the Outline panel.

11. Click to the right of the word *programs* in the last paragraph of the Bully No More slide in the Outline panel.

12. Tap [Ctrl]+[Enter] to create a slide.

13. Type **Kids for Change** in the Outline panel as the slide title, tap [Enter], and then tap [Tab] to create a new, bulleted paragraph.

14. Type **Part of the Solution** in the Outline panel.

15. Choose **Home→Slides→Layout→Section Header**.

16. Scroll to the top of the Outline panel and click anywhere in the text of the first slide to select the slide.

17. Choose **Home→Slides→Layout→Title Slide**.

Copy Formatting

18. Choose **Views→Presentation Views→Normal**.

19. Display slide 4, **Toy Collection**.

20. Select the text *foster homes*.

21. Choose **Home→Font→Bold**.

22. Double-click the **Home→Clipboard→Format Painter** button to load the Format Painter for multiple uses.

23. Click each of the words *emergency, responders, Child,* and *Services* to copy the bold formatting.

24. Choose **Home→Clipboard→Format Painter** to unload the Format Painter.

Organize with Sections

25. Choose **View→Presentation Views→Slide Sorter**.

26. Slide the **Zoom** slider at the bottom-right of the PowerPoint window until all seven slides are visible.

27. Click the **iRecycling Day** slide to select it.

28. Choose **Home→Slides→Section→Add Section** to create a new section.

29. Right-click the untitled section heading and choose **Rename Section**.

30. Type **Community** and then click **Rename**.

31. Click the **Bully No More** slide.

32. Choose **Home→Slides→Section→Add Section**.

33. Right-click the untitled section heading and choose **Rename Section**.

34. Type **School** and then click **Rename**.

35. Drag the **Tutoring** slide to the right of the **Bully No More** slide to move it to the **School** section.

36. Save the presentation.

Print Slides

37. Choose **File→Print** to display the Print tab in Backstage view.

38. Use the scroll bar at the right of the PowerPoint window to navigate the slides until **slide 1** displays.

39. Choose your printer from the **Printer** option. Use the PDF option if specified by your instructor.

40. Specify to print a **Custom Range** of **slides 1–3**; specify **3 slides per page**.

41. Set the color option to **Black and White**; print one copy.

42. Submit your final file based on guidelines provided by your instructor. Exit **PowerPoint**.

Apply Your Skills

Reformat a Presentation

In this exercise, you will create a presentation for Universal Corporate Events based on a Microsoft Word outline. You will then add a slide and format text.

Create a Word Outline

1. Start **Word** and click **Blank Document**.

2. Save the file as **PP02-A01-Outline-[FirstInitialLastName]** in your **PP2013 Lesson 02** folder.

3. Choose **View→Views→Outline**.

4. Type the following text, using ⏎Enter, ⇥Tab, and ⇧Shift+⇥Tab as needed to create an outline in Word.

⊕ Universal Corporate Events
   ⊖ Events made easy
⊕ Event Types
   ⊖ Celebrations
   ⊖ Ceremonies
   ⊖ Team building
   ⊖ Trade shows
⊕ Services
   ⊖ Catering
   ⊖ Invitations
   ⊖ Stage and sound equipment
   ⊖ Venue scouting
⊕ Benefits
   ⊕ Our Jobs
      ⊖ Deal with paperwork
      ⊖ Guarantee safety
      ⊖ Scheduling
   ⊕ Your Jobs
      ⊖ Relax
      ⊖ Enjoy your event
⊕ Universal Corporate Events
   ⊖ Events made easy

5. Save and then close your file. Exit **Word**.

Import a Word Outline

6. Start **PowerPoint** and click **Blank Presentation**.

7. Save your file as `PP02-A01-Outline-[FirstInitialLastName]` to your **PP2013 Lesson 02** folder.

8. Choose **Home→Slides→New Slide→Slides from Outline**.

9. Browse to the **PP2013 Lesson 02** folder and double-click the **PP02-A01-Outline-[FirstInitialLastName]** Word outline.

10. Delete the blank first slide.

Work with an Outline

11. Display the presentation in **Outline View**.

12. Click at the end of the last paragraph of the **Benefits** slide in the Outline panel.

13. Press ⌗Ctrl⌗+⌗Enter⌗ to create a new slide.

14. Type `Specialties`, tap ⌗Enter⌗, and then tap ⌗Tab⌗.

15. Type the following paragraphs, tapping ⌗Enter⌗ after each except the last one.

    ```
    Custom catering
    Individual transportation
    Group transportation
    Line dancing
    Graphic design
    Radio promotion
    Emergency medical
    Large-item printing
    ```

Formatting a Presentation

16. Apply the **Facet** design document theme.

17. Display the presentation in **Normal** view.

18. Ensure that the Specialties slide is displayed and then apply the **Two Content** layout.

19. Select the last four paragraphs on the **Specialties** slide and move them to the new right-column placeholder.

20. Click **slide 1** in the Slides panel and then choose **Home→Slides→Layout→Title Slide**.

21. Click **slide 1** in the Slides panel and then ⌗Shift⌗+click **slide 6** to select all slides.

22. Choose **Home→Slides→Reset**.

23. Display slide 4, **Benefits**.

24. Select the **Our Jobs** paragraph; bold the text.

25. Choose **Home→Font→Character Spacing→Loose** to spread the text out horizontally.

Using the Format Painter

26. Load the **Format Painter** with the formatting.

27. Drag across the *Your Jobs* paragraph to copy the formatting to the paragraph.

28. Save your presentation. Submit your final file based on the guidelines provided by your instructor. Exit **PowerPoint**.

    To view examples of how your file or files should look at the end of this exercise, go to the student resource center.

Organize and Print a Presentation

In this exercise, you will use Slide Sorter view to create sections and organize the slides within a presentation. You will then print a portion of the presentation.

Using the Slide Sorter

1. Start **PowerPoint**. Open **PP02-A02-Outline** from the **PP2013 Lesson 02** folder and save it as `PP02-A02-Outline-[FirstInitialLastName]`.

2. Display the presentation in **Slide Sorter** view.

3. Drag the **Zoom** slider in the lower-right area of the PowerPoint window until you can see all six slides.

Rearranging Slides

4. Drag the **Benefits** slide so that it is after the **Specialties** slide.

5. Drag the **Services** slide so that it is before the **Event Types** slide.

Sections

6. Click the **Services** slide and then add a section.

7. Rename the new section `Services`.

8. Click the **Benefits** slide and then add a section.

9. Rename the new section `Closing`.

10. Save the presentation.

Print a Presentation

11. Choose **File→Print**.

12. Select the **Specialties** slide.

13. Using the **Grayscale** option, print the single slide. Print the slide as a PDF file if directed to do so by your instructor.

14. Close the presentation and exit **PowerPoint**.

15. Submit your final file based on the guidelines provided by your instructor.

    To view examples of how your file or files should look at the end of this exercise, go to the student resource center.

Create, Format, and Organize a Presentation

In this exercise, you will create and import an outline from Word and then design and format a presentation.

Outline in Word

1. Start **Word** and use **Outline View** to create an outline that will produce the following slides:

SLIDES	
Title	**Bullets**
Universal Corporate Events	Specialized
Specialties	▪ Custom catering
	▪ Individual transportation
	▪ Group transportation
	▪ Line dancing
	▪ Graphic design
	▪ Radio promotion
	▪ Emergency medical
	▪ Large-item printing
Catering	▪ Vegan dishes
	▪ Kosher dishes
	▪ Meat-lovers dishes
	▪ Desserts
Transportation	▪ Individual limos
	▪ Group buses for 6-50
Line Dancing	▪ Experienced dance leaders
	▪ Country, pop, and hip-hop
Graphic Design	▪ Invitation graphics
	▪ Signs
	▪ Banners
Radio Promotion	▪ Script writing
	▪ Voice talent
	▪ High-definition recording
Emergency Medical	▪ CPR-certified staff
	▪ Onsite portable defibrillators
Large-Item Printing	▪ Canvas, polyester, or vinyl
	▪ Up to 64 square feet

2. Save the outline to your **PP2013 Lesson 02** folder as `PP02-A03-Outline-[FirstInitialLastName]` and close Word.

3. Start **PowerPoint** and create a new, blank presentation in the **PP2013 Lesson 02** folder named `PP02-A03-Outline-[FirstInitialLastName]`.

4. Import the **PP02-A03-Outline-[FirstInitialLastName]** Word outline.

5. Delete the blank first slide.

PowerPoint 2013

Work with Slides and Formatting

6. Select all slides in the Slides panel and use the **Reset** command to reset the formatting.

7. Apply the **Ion Boardroom** theme with the **orange variation**.

8. Change the layout of the first slide to **Title Slide**.

9. Change the layout of the second slide to **Two Content**.

10. Move the last four paragraphs of the second slide into the new right-column placeholder.

11. Increase the line spacing of both columns on **slide 2** to **2.0**.

Work with an Outline

12. Display the presentation in **Outline View**.

13. Collapse all the slides on the Outline panel.

14. Select the **Specialties** slide in the Outline panel and then expand only that one slide.

15. In the Outline panel, move the *Large-item printing* paragraph below the *Graphic design* paragraph.

16. In the Outline panel, move the *Large-Item Printing* slide below the **Graphic Design** slide.

17. Display the presentation in **Normal** view.

Formatting a Presentation

18. Display the **Catering** slide.

19. Make the word *Vegan* bold and italic and then use the **Format Painter** to copy the formatting to the words *Kosher* and *Meat-lovers*.

20. Change the case of all eight paragraphs on the **Specialties** slide to **Capitalize Each Word**.

Using the Slide Sorter

21. Display the presentation in **Slide Sorter** view.

22. Create a new section starting with **slide 1** named `Intro`.

23. Create a new section starting with the **Catering** slide named `Food and Entertainment`.

24. Create a new section starting with the **Transportation** slide named `Logistics and Emergency`.

25. Create a new section starting with the **Graphic Design** slide named `Promotion`.

26. Move the **Line Dancing** slide to the end of the **Food and Entertainment** section.

27. Move the **Emergency Medical** slide to the end of the **Logistics and Emergency** section.

28. Move the entire **Promotion** section so that it is before the **Logistics and Emergency** section.

29. Save the presentation.

Print a Presentation

30. Print the slides in the **Promotion** section in the **Handouts (3 slides per page)** format so that only a single page prints. Print in **Grayscale** to save on color ink. (Or print to PDF if instructed to by your instructor.)

31. Submit your final file based on the instructions provided by your instructor. Exit **PowerPoint**.

Extend Your Skills

In the course of working through the Extend Your Skills exercises, you will think critically as you use the skills taught in the lesson to complete the assigned projects. To evaluate your mastery and completion of the exercises, your instructor may use a rubric, with which more points are allotted according to performance characteristics. (The more you do, the more you earn!) Ask your instructor how your work will be evaluated.

PP02-E01 That's the Way I See It

You're teaching a cooking class and need a presentation to show others how to make your signature dish. Choose a recipe that you know well, or find one online. When you're ready, create a new presentation named **PP02-E01-Recipe-[FirstInitialLastName]** in your **PP2013 Lesson 02** folder.

Apply the design theme and variation of your choice. If you can't find a design theme you like, use PowerPoint's Start screen to search for others. Type the recipe name as the slide title and create an engaging subtitle. Add a Title and Content slide that lists the ingredients. Create at least three more slides, each of which describes a few fun facts about one of the ingredients (look it up or make it up).

Add a slide that lists a brief description of each step. Each paragraph should contain no more than four words. Create an additional slide for each step, using the brief description as the slide title and bulleted paragraphs to further explain the step. Copy the brief descriptions one by one and paste them onto the additional slides. Create an **Ingredients** section that contains all the ingredient slides and a **Steps** section that includes all the step slides.

Run the slide show and make note of anything you want to change. When the slide show ends, make the necessary changes and then save your presentation. You will be evaluated based on the inclusion of all elements specified, your ability to follow directions, your ability to apply newly learned skills to a real-world situation, your creativity, and the relevance of your topic and/or data choice(s). Submit your final file based on the guidelines provided by your instructor.

PP02-E02 Be Your Own Boss

Open **PP02-E02-BlueJean** from the **PP2013 Lesson 02** folder and save it as **PP02-E02-BlueJean-[FirstInitialLastName]**. View the presentation as a slide show and ask yourself if the slides are easy to read and in the best order. Based on your evaluation, use the skills taught in this lesson to make the necessary changes, ensuring that you cover these edits.

- Change the document theme.
- Adjust the text layout.
- Rearrange the order of slides.
- Edit text.

Be sure the design and formatting are consistent from slide to slide. Use the Format Painter to quickly duplicate formatting changes. Add at least three more slides, such as those to describe Blue Jean Landscaping products, a brief company history, or a price list. Rearrange the slides and create at least two sections to group slides in a logical order.

You will be evaluated based on the inclusion of all elements specified, your ability to follow directions, your ability to apply newly learned skills to a real-world situation, your creativity, and your demonstration of an entrepreneurial spirit. Submit your final file based on the guidelines provided by your instructor.

Transfer Your Skills

In the course of working through the Transfer Your Skills exercises, you will use critical-thinking and creativity skills to complete the assigned projects using skills taught in the lesson. To evaluate your mastery and completion of the exercises, your instructor may use a rubric, with which more points are allotted according to performance characteristics. (The more you do, the more you earn!) Ask your instructor how your work will be evaluated.

PP02-T01 Use the Web as a Learning Tool

Throughout this book, you will be provided with an opportunity to use the Internet as a learning tool by completing WebQuests. According to the original creators of WebQuests, as described on their website (WebQuest.org), a WebQuest is "an inquiry-oriented activity in which most or all of the information used by learners is drawn from the web." To complete the WebQuest projects in this book, navigate to the student resource center and choose the WebQuest for the lesson on which you are currently working. The subject of each WebQuest will be relevant to the material found in the lesson.

WebQuest Subject: Designing an Effective Presentation

Submit your final file(s) based on the guidelines provided by your instructor.

PP02-T02 Demonstrate Proficiency

Stormy BBQ is sponsoring a Father's Day picnic. Create a PowerPoint presentation to display on the widescreen monitors at Stormy's to play during business hours that gives details about the event.

Create an outline in Microsoft Word that will produce at least five slides when imported into PowerPoint. The slides should describe the picnic and various events and entertainment. Save the Word outline as **PP02-T02-FathersDay-[FirstInitialLastName]** to your **PP2013 Lesson 02** folder.

Import the outline into PowerPoint to create the initial slides. Use an appropriate theme and change the slide layouts as necessary. Format the text so important words stand out, but be careful not to overdo it! Experiment with character and line spacing, paragraph alignment, and other formatting. Use the Format Painter to quickly reuse preferred formatting. Create sections for different parts of the event, such as for food, games, and other activities.

Save your presentation as **PP02-T02-FathersDay-[FirstInitialLastName]** in your **PP2013 Lesson 02** folder.

Submit your final file based on the guidelines provided by your instructor.

POWERPOINT 2013

Adding Graphics, Animation, and Sound

LEARNING OBJECTIVES

After studying this lesson, you will be able to:

- Add clip art, photos, screenshots, and shapes to a presentation
- Remove backgrounds and apply artistic effects to slide images
- Add transition effects to a slide show
- Add animation to objects on a slide
- Add sound effects to transitions and animations

In this lesson, you will enhance a presentation that currently includes only text. You will use online clip art to add interest to the presentation, a drawing object to add spark, and slide transitions and animation to "bring the presentation to life."

Adding Eye Candy

The iJams presentation is evolving nicely. However, you know you will have to add some pizzazz to it if iJams is to contend with competitors. Although you have created an error-free, technically perfect presentation, you can see that something is definitely missing! You decide that if used sparingly, clip art and animation will enhance the presentation.

The iJams presentation with stock clip art added

Working with Online Pictures

Video Library   http://labyrinthelab.com/videos   Video Number: PP13-V0301

You can search for and insert clip art from the Internet directly from within PowerPoint. Adding clip art will help you emphasize key points and add polish to the presentation as a whole. The Microsoft Office website has a clip art collection of more than 130,000 pieces of art—and it grows daily. There is clip art available for any occasion.

While the term *clip art* is an industry-standard term referring to predrawn artwork that is added to computer documents, Microsoft uses the terms *clip art* and *online pictures* inconsistently to refer to the same thing. For example, PowerPoint's Online Pictures button opens the Insert Pictures dialog box, which allows you to search the Office.com website for clip art.

Using Text and Object Layouts

PowerPoint creates slides with different layouts, such as slides with titles only and slides with titles and text. These slide layouts allow you to easily create slides with a standardized title and bulleted text. Many of PowerPoint's layouts, including the Title and Content layout and the Two Content layout, provide placeholders for titles, text, and various types of content including tables, charts, clip art from the Internet, pictures from your computer, organizational charts, and movies.

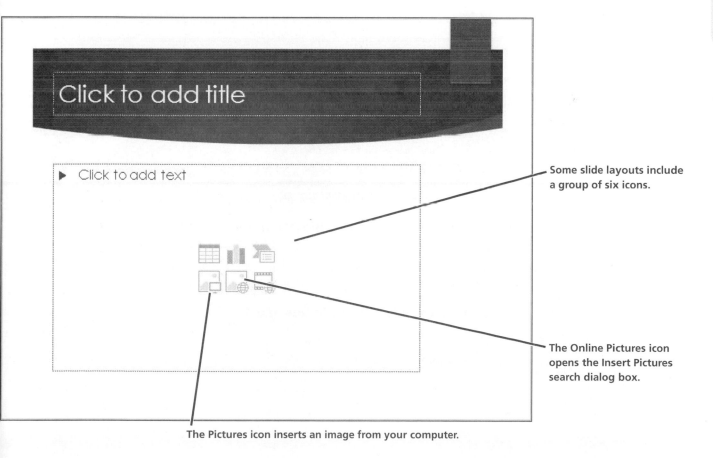

Some slide layouts include a group of six icons.

The Online Pictures icon opens the Insert Pictures search dialog box.

The Pictures icon inserts an image from your computer.

PowerPoint 2013

Icon	What It Does	Icon	What It Does
	Inserts a table		Inserts an image
	Inserts a chart or graph		Inserts a SmartArt graphic
	Opens the Online Pictures dialog box to insert clip art		Inserts a video clip

Deleting Placeholder Text

Sometimes you may decide to replace all text on a slide with a graphic. Deleting all text inside a placeholder results in the slide displaying its six default insert icons, making it easy to insert clip art or other objects.

Many successes

Record sales

When all the text inside a placeholder is deleted...

Click to add text

...the six insert icons reappear.

Get a Slide Ready for Clip Art

In this exercise, you will get a slide ready to accept clip art.

1. Start **PowerPoint**. Open **PP03-D01-Animation** from the **PP2013 Lesson 03** folder, and save it as **PP03-D01-Animation-[FirstInitialLastName]**.

    Replace the bracketed text with your first initial and last name. For example, if your name is Bethany Smith, your filename would look like this: PP03-D01-Animation-BSmith.

2. Select the **Our Services** slide from the **Slides panel**.

3. Choose **Home→Slides→New Slide** .

    A new slide is inserted below Our Services. The new slide uses the same layout as the Our Services slide.

Choose a Layout and Format Text

4. Follow these steps to apply a slide layout suitable for clip art:

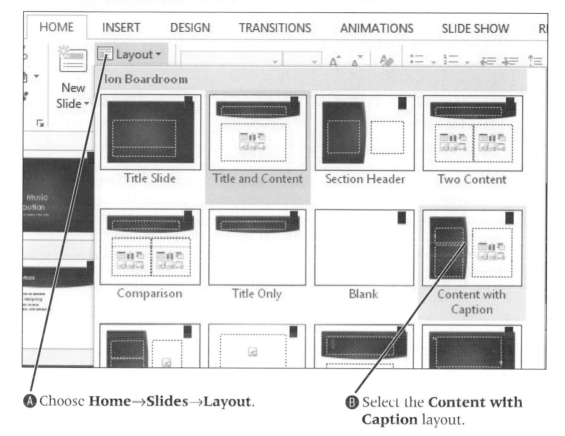

A Choose **Home→Slides→Layout**.

B Select the **Content with Caption** layout.

5. In the Title placeholder, type `Our Recent Success`.

6. In the text box beneath the title, type:

`Top of the Rock` `Enter` `Excellence in Service to Musicians` `Enter`
`League of Electronic Music Distributors.`

7. Select the text *Top of the Rock;* choose **Home→Font→Font Size menu ▼** and then choose **24**.

8. Choose **Home→Font→Bold**.

9. Select the text *League of Electronic Music Distributors.*

10. Choose **Home→Font→Italic**.

Your slide is ready for clip art.

11. Click in the large text placeholder at the right and type:

`Many successes` `Enter`
`Record-breaking sales`

You decide instead to replace the bulleted text with clip art. You will delete all the text in the placeholder so the slide displays the six insert icons again.

12. Click inside the text box, if necessary, to display its dashed border.

13. Click the dashed border to select the text box.

14. Tap Delete .

The text is deleted, and the six insert icons reappear.

15. Save your presentation.

Searching for Clip Art with the Insert Pictures Search Window

Video Library   http://labyrinthelab.com/videos   Video Number: PP13-V0302

The Insert Pictures search window replaces the Clip Art panel that existed in previous versions of PowerPoint. This new window lets you search for clip art on the Office.com Clip Art website or from the Bing™ search engine. Each piece of clip art is associated with keywords that describe its characteristics. The first illustration that follows describes the Insert Pictures search window. The second illustration shows the images that can be located by using the keyword *awards* or *prizes*.

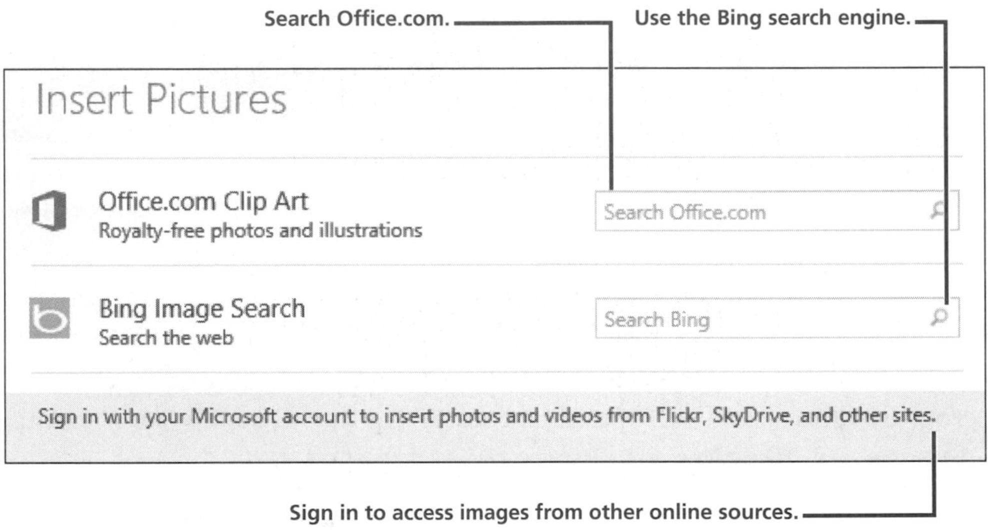

Begin a new search from a different search engine. View a larger version of the image.

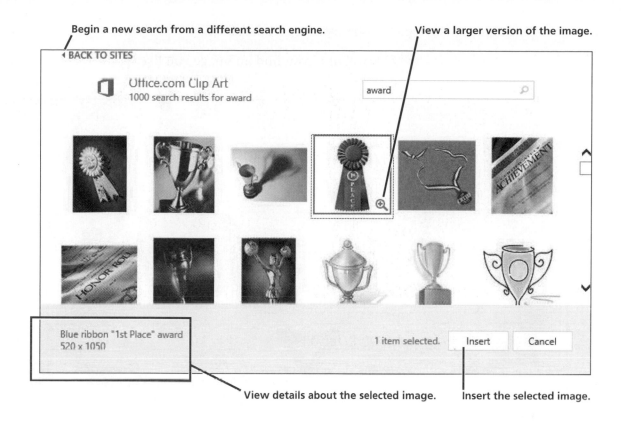

View details about the selected image. Insert the selected image.

DEVELOP YOUR SKILLS PP03-D02

Insert Clip Art

In this exercise, you will insert clip art to add visual interest to a slide.

1. Save your file as **PP03-D02-Animation-[FirstInitialLastName]**.

2. On the **Our Recent Success** slide, click the **Online Pictures** icon to open the Insert Pictures search window.

3. Type **award** in the Office.com search box and then tap Enter.

4. Follow these steps to insert a picture on the slide:

Ⓐ Scroll until you find an image you like.
Your results may differ from the figure.

Ⓑ Click an image to select it.

Ⓒ Click **Insert**.

The clip art image is inserted on the slide and replaces the large text box.

5. Save the presentation.

Moving, Sizing, and Rotating Objects

Video Library   http://labyrinthelab.com/videos   Video Number: PP13-V0303

When you click an object (such as a clip art image), sizing handles and a rotate handle appear. You can easily move, size, and rotate the selected object.

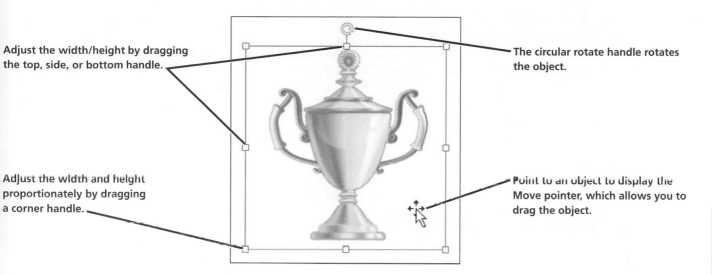

Adjust the width/height by dragging the top, side, or bottom handle.

The circular rotate handle rotates the object.

Adjust the width and height proportionately by dragging a corner handle.

Point to an object to display the Move pointer, which allows you to drag the object.

Stacking Objects

Sometimes when you insert a picture, it overlaps text or some other object. You can change the stacking order of objects, such as pictures and shapes, by moving them forward or backward.

If an object is covering text...

...send it behind the text.

Task	Procedure
Move an object back one object at a time	Select the object and then choose Picture Tools→Format→Arrange→Send Backward.
Move an object up one object at a time	Select the object and then choose Picture Tools→Format→Arrange→Bring Forward.
Move an object to the very back of a slide	Select the object and then choose Picture Tools→Format→Arrange→Send Backward ▼→Send to Back.
Move an object to the very front of a slide	Select the object and then choose Picture Tools→Format→Arrange→Bring Forward ▼→Bring to Front.

DEVELOP YOUR SKILLS PP03-D03

Move and Size Clip Art

In this exercise, you will manipulate clip art, sizing and moving it to place it on the slide.

1. Save your file as **PP03-D03-Animation-[FirstInitialLastName]**.

2. Follow these steps to rotate the clip art image:

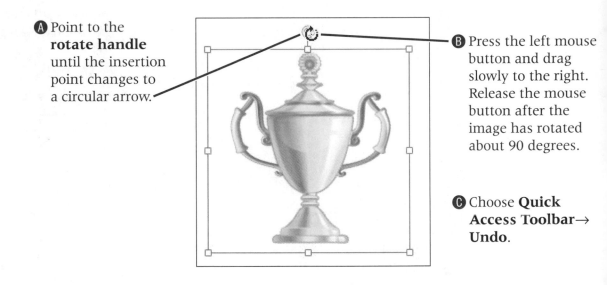

Ⓐ Point to the **rotate handle** until the insertion point changes to a circular arrow.

Ⓑ Press the left mouse button and drag slowly to the right. Release the mouse button after the image has rotated about 90 degrees.

Ⓒ Choose **Quick Access Toolbar→ Undo**.

3. Follow these steps to resize the clip art image:

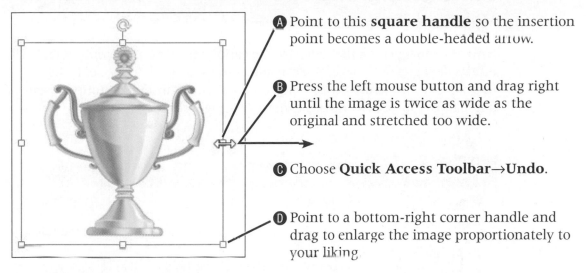

Ⓐ Point to this **square handle** so the insertion point becomes a double-headed arrow.

Ⓑ Press the left mouse button and drag right until the image is twice as wide as the original and stretched too wide.

Ⓒ Choose **Quick Access Toolbar→Undo**.

Ⓓ Point to a bottom-right corner handle and drag to enlarge the image proportionately to your liking.

4. Point to the image itself (not the border or a resize handle) until the pointer becomes a four-headed arrow. Drag so the image is centered next to the bar of text.

Compare your slide to the following illustration.

5. Save your presentation.

Formatting Clip Art

Video Library   http://labyrinthelab.com/videos   Video Number: PP13-V0304

After your image is on the slide, use the various groups on the contextual Format tab to add effects or align your image. You can add borders, drop-shadows, or bevels, or rotate your image in 3-D from the Picture Styles group on the Format tab. Other groups on this tab allow you to align, flip, crop, or perform basic image-editing tasks.

QUICK REFERENCE	PERFORMING CLIP ART TASKS
Task	**Procedure**
Insert a clip art image from an online source	■ Click the Online Pictures shortcut 🖼 or choose Insert→Images→Online Pictures. ■ Enter a search term and tap [Enter]. ■ Click the desired thumbnail and then click Insert.
Insert an image from your computer	■ Click the Pictures shortcut 🖼 or choose Insert→Images→Pictures. ■ Browse your computer's location for an image. ■ Click the desired image and then click Insert.
Resize a clip art image	■ Click the clip art image to display its border. ■ Drag any square handle along the top, bottom, or sides of the clip art's border to resize the image wider or taller. ■ Drag any handle in the clip art's corners to resize the image proportionately.
Move a clip art image	■ Point to the image until the mouse pointer becomes a four-headed arrow. ■ Drag the image to the desired location.
Rotate a clip art image	■ Click the clip art image to display its border. ■ Point to the rotate handle above the clip art's top border until the mouse pointer becomes a circular arrow. ■ Drag left or right to rotate the image.
Format a clip art image	■ Click the clip art image to display its border. ■ Choose Format→Picture Styles and then choose a command.

DEVELOP YOUR SKILLS PP03-D04

Insert and Format Clip Art

In this exercise, you will work with the Ribbon to insert and format an image on your slide.

1. Save your file as **PP03-D04-Animation-[FirstInitialLastName]**.

2. Display the **title slide**.

3. Choose **Insert→Images→Online Pictures** 🖼.

4. Follow these steps to insert clip art on the title slide:

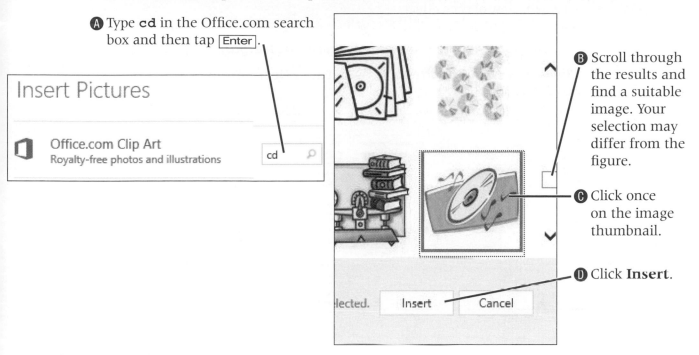

Ⓐ Type **cd** in the Office.com search box and then tap Enter.

Ⓑ Scroll through the results and find a suitable image. Your selection may differ from the figure.

Ⓒ Click once on the image thumbnail.

Ⓓ Click **Insert**.

Size and Position the Image

Next, you will use the Format contextual tab to experiment with effect options.

5. Drag the image to the top of the slide so it no longer overlaps the text. Then drag the top-right corner handle toward the top-right corner of your slide to enlarge the image proportionately.

Be careful not to size it too large; the image should still fit on the slide.

6. Choose **Format→Arrange→Align→Align Center**.

Selecting an image object forces the display of the contextual Format tab.

7. Make sure the image displays handles to indicate it is selected and then choose **Format→Picture Styles→Picture Effects**.

8. Roll your insertion point over several of the items in the **Picture Effects** gallery to view a Live Preview of each effect.

As you have seen with other commands, Live Preview makes it easy to anticipate the effect of a command without the need to undo it if you don't like the effect.

9. Choose **Format→Picture Styles→Picture Effects→Glow→Gold, 18 pt glow, Accent color 3**.

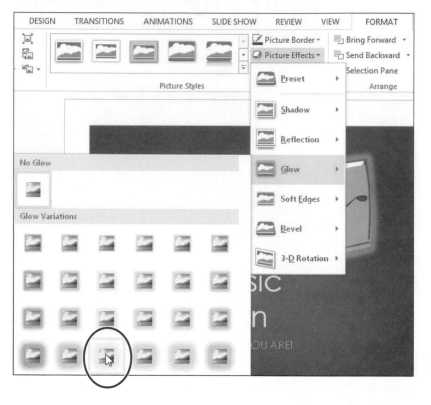

PowerPoint applies a glowing effect to the edge of the image.

10. If necessary, resize and move your image so it doesn't overlap the text.

11. Save your presentation.

Adding Other Graphics

Video Library   http://labyrinthelab.com/videos   Video Number: PP13-V0305

Sometimes you just can't find that perfect image through clip art. Often you can incorporate more-unique and personal imagery if you take your own pictures or download professional photographs from a commercial website. PowerPoint 2013 includes tools and features to make the most of your images, including the ability to remove a background and add artistic effects.

Removing a Background

Many times a photograph contains more than what you need. In the past, it was necessary to use a graphics-editing program to remove the background or other unwanted elements. PowerPoint 2013 includes a feature that allows you to remove backgrounds with just a few clicks. When removing a background, the original picture is not harmed, because PowerPoint works on a copy of the picture embedded in the slide. Additionally, nothing is actually removed from the picture. PowerPoint just hides areas of the picture that you mark to be removed. The hidden areas can always be made visible again. You can adjust the settings of the removal tool at any time after the background's initial removal, so there is no need to worry about getting it perfect on your first try.

The Background Removal tool overlays in purple the areas to be removed.

With just a few clicks, the background can be removed.

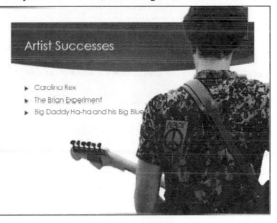

PowerPoint 2013

DEVELOP YOUR SKILLS PP03-D05

Remove a Background

In this exercise, you will insert a picture and remove the background.

1. Save your file as **PP03-D05-Animation-[FirstInitialLastName]**.

2. Scroll down the Slides pane, if necessary, and select the **Artist Successes** slide.

3. Choose **Insert→Images→Pictures**.

4. Navigate to your **PP2013 Lesson 03** folder, select the **PP03-D05-Guitarist** picture, and click **Insert**.

   The picture is inserted on the slide, but contains more imagery than we need.

Remove the Background

5. Drag the picture up so its top snaps to the top of the slide.

6. Drag the bottom handle down until the bottom of the picture snaps to the bottom of the slide.

   The picture now covers the whole slide.

7. Choose **Picture Tools→Format→Adjust→Remove Background**.

   PowerPoint places a rectangular border inside the picture and does its best to guess what you want to remove. A purple overlay indicates the content that will be removed. You will adjust this.

8. Drag the top-right handle of the rectangular box inside the picture so it snaps to the top-right corner of the picture.

9. Drag the bottom-left handle of the rectangular box down and right so the entire guitar is inside the box.

   Your slide should resemble the following figure, but it will not be exact.

   When you resize the box inside the picture, PowerPoint adjusts the purple overlay. The overlay still needs to be adjusted so you can see the whole guitarist.

10. Choose **Background Removal→Refine→Mark Areas to Keep**.

11. Follow these steps to adjust the overlay:

Ⓐ Point to the top of the left shoulder and drag down to the bottom of the elbow to tell PowerPoint not to remove this area.

Ⓑ Point to the left edge of the guitar and drag right to keep this area.

Ⓒ Drag over any other purple on the guitarist or the guitar.

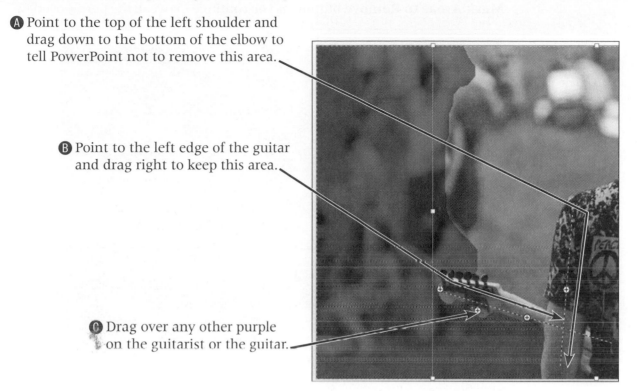

12. Choose **Background Removal→Refine→Mark Areas to Remove**.

13. Follow these steps to define areas to be removed:

Ⓐ Drag over the background to tell PowerPoint to remove this area.

Ⓑ Drag over this section to remove it as well.

14. You will probably have to go back and forth with the **Mark Areas to Keep** and **Mark Areas to Remove** buttons as you continue to tweak the purple overlay.

15. Choose **Background Removal→Close→Keep Changes**.

16. Drag the image to the right so all three bulleted paragraphs are visible. If your slide doesn't resemble the following figure, choose **Picture Tools→Format→Adjust→Remove Background** to adjust the overlay.

Part of the image extends to the right beyond the slide. While it may look strange in Normal view, it will look fine as a slide show. The areas outside the slide will not display.

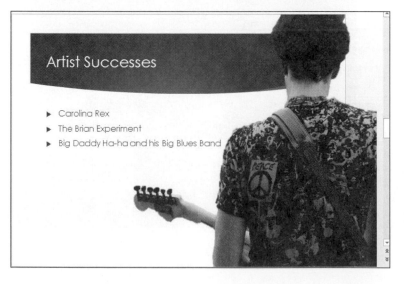

17. Save your presentation.

Applying Artistic Effects

Video Library   http://labyrinthelab.com/videos   Video Number: PP13-V0306

PowerPoint 2013 includes artistic effects that can be applied to pictures, making photographs look like pencil sketches, cement, or pastels. Additionally, pictures can be recolored to create a color cast that blends with your theme.

The picture before any effect has been applied

The picture after the Pencil Sketch and Recolor effects have been applied

QUICK REFERENCE	MODIFYING PICTURES
Task	**Procedure**
Remove a background	■ Select the picture and choose Picture Tools→Format→Adjust→Remove Background.
	■ Adjust the marquee to include the portion of the picture you want to keep.
	■ Choose Background Removal→Refine→Mark Areas to Keep and drag over additional areas to include.
	■ Choose Background Removal→Refine→Mark Areas to Remove and drag over additional areas to exclude.
	■ Choose Background Removal→Refine→Keep Changes.
	■ Choose Picture Tools→Format→Adjust→Remove Background to adjust the background removal at any time.
Apply artistic effects	■ Select the picture and choose Picture Tools→Format→Adjust→Artistic Effects.
	■ Choose an effect to apply the default settings, or choose Artistic Effects Options to customize the settings.
	■ If you choose to customize, choose an effect from the drop-down menu, adjust the settings, and click Close.

Apply Artistic Effects

In this exercise, you will apply artistic effects to a picture to enhance its visual appeal.

1. Save your file as **PP03-D06-Animation-[FirstInitialLastName]**.

2. If necessary, select the picture on the sixth slide, **Artistic Successes**.

3. Choose **Picture Tools→Format→Adjust→Artistic Effects**.

4. Point to several effects to see how they change the picture on the slide. Notice that a ToolTip appears when you point to an effect, indicating its name.

5. Select the **Pencil Grayscale** effect.

6. Choose **Picture Tools→Format→Adjust→Color**.

7. Point to several color adjustments to see how they change the picture on the slide. *Notice the ToolTip that appears.*

8. Select the **Teal, Accent Color 5 Light** adjustment.

9. Save your presentation.

Inserting a Screenshot

Video Library   http://labyrinthelab.com/videos   Video Number: PP13-V0307

Sometimes you may want to include a picture of something on your computer screen, such as a program window or web page, in a presentation. PowerPoint's Screenshot tool lets you insert a picture of any open window or program or drag on your screen to define an area to insert.

The Screenshot command is available on the Insert tab.

You can insert any open window as a picture.

You can drag on the screen to define an area to capture.

QUICK REFERENCE	INSERTING A SCREENSHOT
Task	**Procedure**
Insert a picture of an entire program window	■ Start the program or open the window you want to capture. ■ Return to PowerPoint and choose the desired slide. ■ Choose Insert→Images→Screenshot menu ▼→desired screenshot.
Insert a picture of a portion of the screen	■ Display the program or window you wish to insert. ■ Return to PowerPoint and choose the desired slide. ■ Choose Insert→Images→Screenshot menu ▼→Screen Clipping. ■ Drag to define the area you wish to insert, or tap [Esc] to leave the Screen Clipping tool.

Working with Shapes

Video Library   http://labyrinthelab.com/videos   Video Number: PP13-V0308

PowerPoint offers more than 150 shapes that you can add to your slides. You can use these shapes to build your own custom flowcharts, mathematical equations, speech and thought bubbles, or other design. Shapes can even include text.

PowerPoint 2013

The Smiley Face and Cloud Callout shapes were used to build this graphic.

Shapes include mathematical symbols.

Shapes are automatically formatted to match the slide's theme.

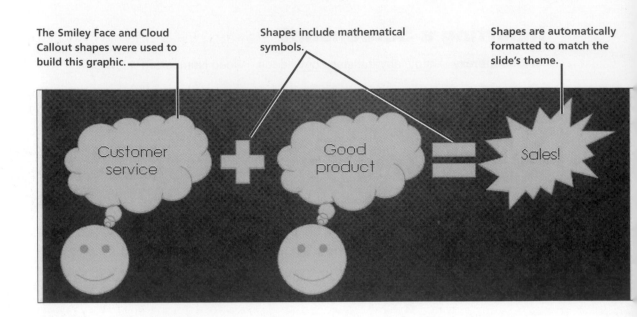

Adding a Shape

When adding a shape to a slide, you can stretch it to make it wider/narrower or taller/shorter. All shapes are preformatted with a specific ratio of width to height, so stretching a shape can sometimes make it appear unbalanced. You can use the Shift key to maintain the original width-to-height ratio.

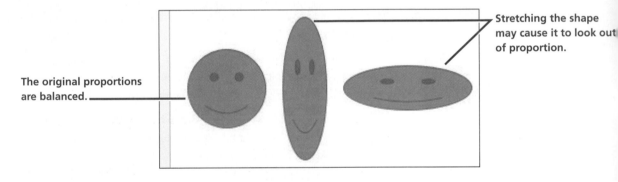

The original proportions are balanced.

Stretching the shape may cause it to look out of proportion.

Adding Text to a Shape

You can easily add text to a shape, but the text does not automatically resize itself to fit nicely. Text will, however, automatically wrap to the next line so there is no need to tap Enter as you type.

Text will automatically wrap to the next line but will not automatically get smaller to fit inside the shape.

You may need to adjust the text size to get it to fit.

Task	Procedure
Add a shape	■ Choose Insert→Illustrations→Shapes ▼.
	■ Select the desired shape and then drag on the slide to draw the shape.
	■ Hold [Shift] as you drag the shape to maintain the original proportions.
Add text to a shape	■ Add a shape to a slide.
	■ With the shape selected and displaying a solid border, start typing.

Resizing a Shape

Shapes can be resized and rotated just like clip art. Additionally, some shapes include a yellow square that you can use to change the shape's properties. For example, you can change the Smiley Face shape to a frown or you can change the head and body of an arrow shape.

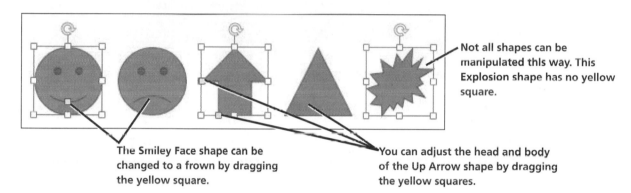

The Smiley Face shape can be changed to a frown by dragging the yellow square.

You can adjust the head and body of the Up Arrow shape by dragging the yellow squares.

Not all shapes can be manipulated this way. This Explosion shape has no yellow square.

Merging Shapes

New in PowerPoint is the ability to merge shapes. This feature allows you to create your own custom shape by combining existing shapes into a single one. The benefit of this is that your new custom shape has a single outline and truly looks like a single shape rather than several overlapped shapes.

The Merge Shapes command is available from the Drawing Tools→Format tab.

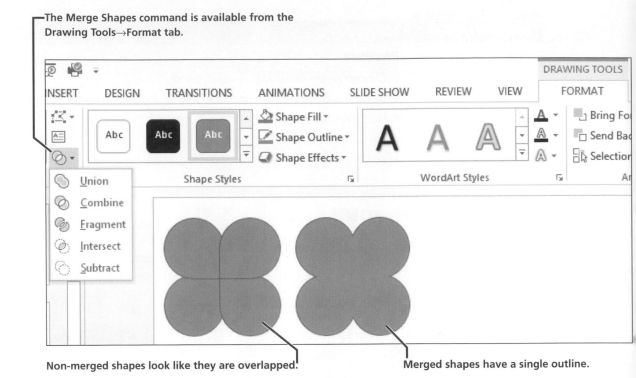

Non-merged shapes look like they are overlapped.

Merged shapes have a single outline.

Formatting Shapes and Shape Text

While shapes and the text they contain are automatically formatted to match the slide's theme, you may want a more exciting look such as a drop-shadow or three-dimensional effect. Adding a Shape Style or WordArt Style can make your shape graphics really pop.

This is the original shape and text.

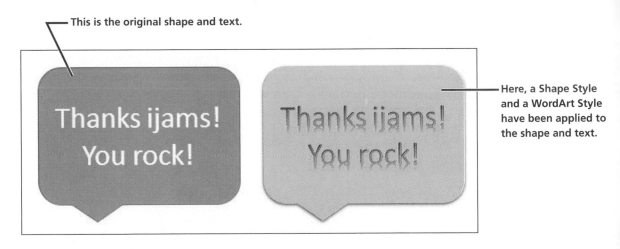

Here, a Shape Style and a WordArt Style have been applied to the shape and text.

Task	Procedure
Format a shape	▪ Select the desired shape.
	▪ Choose a command from Drawing Tools→Format→Shape Styles.
Format shape text	▪ Select the desired shape.
	▪ Choose a command from Drawing Tools→Format→WordArt Styles.

DEVELOP YOUR SKILLS PP03-D07
Add and Format a Shape with Text

In this exercise, you will add and format a shape with text.

1. Save your file as **PP03-D07-Animation-[FirstInitialLastName]**.

2. Display the seventh slide, **Carolina Rex**.

3. Choose **Insert→Illustrations→Shapes ▼→Stars and Banners→5-Point Star**.

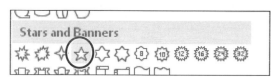

4. Hold [Shift] as you drag on the slide to create a star shape.

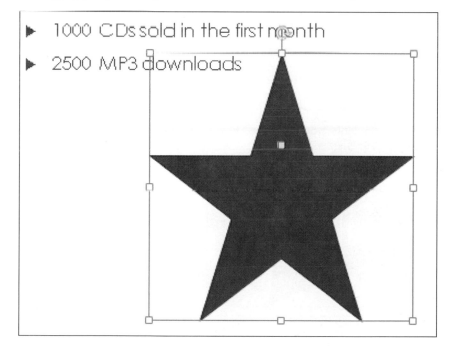

PowerPoint 2013

5. Type the following: `Top Seller!`

Your star shape should resemble this figure, though your text may fit on a single line.

6. Click the dashed border of the shape so it turns solid.

When the shape is selected, you can format its text.

7. Choose **Home→Font→Font Size ▼→44**.

The font size increases, but the text no longer fits nicely inside the shape. You will fix this in the next few steps.

Customize the Shape

8. Follow these steps to change the shape of the star and make the text fit nicely:

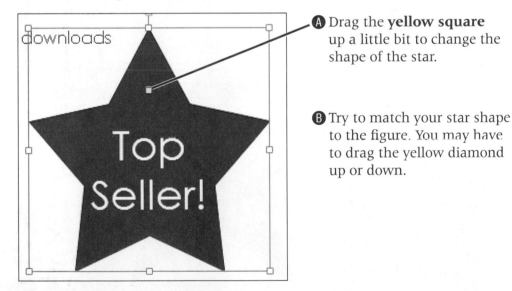

Ⓐ Drag the **yellow square** up a little bit to change the shape of the star.

Ⓑ Try to match your star shape to the figure. You may have to drag the yellow diamond up or down.

Format the Shape and Text

9. Choose **Drawing Tools→Format→Shape Styles→More→Intense Effect – Purple, Accent 6**

    The shape changes color and appears three-dimensional. However, the text remains the same.

10. Choose **Drawing Tools→Format→WordArt Styles→More→Fill – White, Outline – Accent 1, Shadow**.

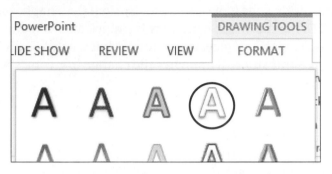

The text within the shape changes.

11. If necessary, change the size of the star shape so the text fits on two lines.

12. Save your presentation.

PowerPoint 2013

Working with Slide Transitions

Video Library   http://labyrinthelab.com/videos   Video Number: PP13-V0309

A slide transition is the animation between slides. Used properly, these transitions can add zest and excitement to your presentation and provide a distinct breaking point between slides. PowerPoint 2013 includes many transitions that are often used in video production, such as 3-D rotations and other animated effects.

The Vortex transition occurring between two slides

Consistency within a presentation helps keep the audience focused. Avoid using different transitions within a single presentation.

Creating Transitions in Slide Sorter View

Most of the time, you will want to apply the same transition to the entire presentation. Maintaining a consistent transition style looks more professional (less haphazard) and is less distracting for the audience. Using the Slide Sorter view is a quick and easy way to accomplish this task. You can apply transitions to a single slide, multiple slides, or all slides in a presentation. When you apply a transition, it animates the change from one slide to another, not individual elements of the slide.

Selecting Slides for Transitions

To easily select all slides in a presentation from Slide Sorter view, click to select any slide and then press Ctrl+A. All slides will be selected. Then, choose Transitions→Transitions to This Slide and select a transition effect. The transition will be applied to all selected slides. You can also use this method from the Normal view's Slides panel to select all slides in a presentation.

To apply a transition to a single slide, select a single slide in either Normal or Slide Sorter view and then choose a slide transition. The transition will be applied to the selected slide.

The Transitions Tab

The Transitions tab contains the Transitions to This Slide group, which you use to implement your slide transitions. The Transitions tab contains commands to apply transitions, sound, and other transition options.

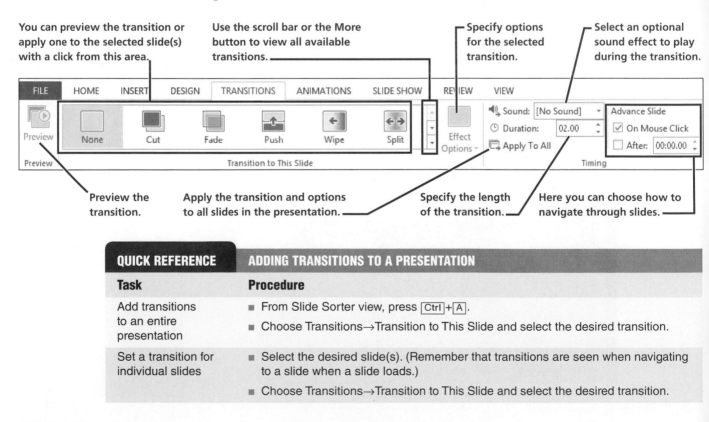

QUICK REFERENCE	ADDING TRANSITIONS TO A PRESENTATION
Task	**Procedure**
Add transitions to an entire presentation	▪ From Slide Sorter view, press Ctrl+A. ▪ Choose Transitions→Transition to This Slide and select the desired transition.
Set a transition for individual slides	▪ Select the desired slide(s). (Remember that transitions are seen when navigating to a slide when a slide loads.) ▪ Choose Transitions→Transition to This Slide and select the desired transition.

Apply Transition Effects

In this exercise, you will apply a transition to all slides except the title slide to make the slide show more interesting.

Choose Transition Effects

1. Save your file as **PP03-D08-Animation-[FirstInitialLastName]**.

2. Choose **View→Presentation Views→Slide Sorter** 🔲.

3. Choose the **Transitions** tab.

4. Click the **Our Services** slide to select it.

5. Use ⌈Shift⌉+click on the **Contact Us** slide.
    Slides 2–11 are selected.

6. Follow these steps to apply a transition effect to the selected slides:

Ⓑ Choose **Vortex**. A preview of the transition appears on each slide.

Ⓐ Click the **More** button and locate the Exciting category.

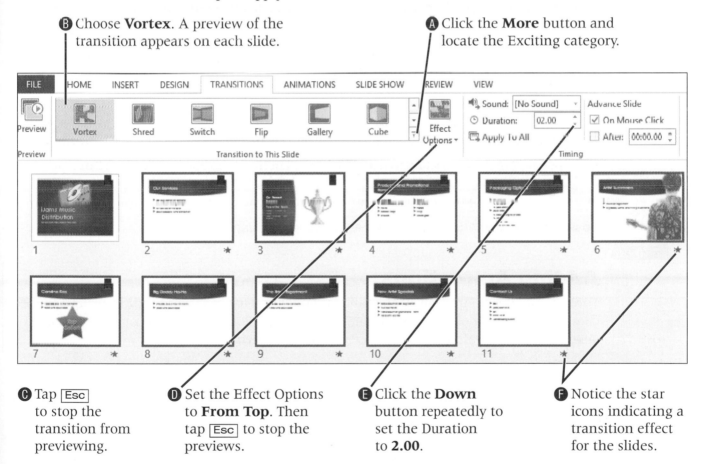

Ⓒ Tap ⌈Esc⌉ to stop the transition from previewing.

Ⓓ Set the Effect Options to **From Top**. Then tap ⌈Esc⌉ to stop the previews.

Ⓔ Click the **Down** button repeatedly to set the Duration to **2.00**.

Ⓕ Notice the star icons indicating a transition effect for the slides.

The title slide does not have the star icon because there is no transition applied to it.

PowerPoint 2013

Run the Presentation

7. Choose **Slide Show→Start Slide Show→From Beginning** [icon].

   The title slide appears without a transition. The title slide would have opened with the Vortex transition if you had applied the transition to it.

8. Click the mouse button to advance to the next slide.

   The Vortex transition effect displays as the slides advance.

9. Continue to click the mouse button until you reach the end of the presentation and the Slide Sorter window reappears.

10. Save your presentation.

Using Slide Animation

Video Library   http://labyrinthelab.com/videos   Video Number: PP13-V0310

Whereas transitions are applied to slides as a whole, animations are applied to individual objects *within* a slide. Animations begin only after any transition effect is completed. Some examples of animation include the following:

■ A clip art image that moves across the slide to its final location

■ A slide that starts out empty, and then has a title and other elements that fade into view with a mouse click

■ Bulleted paragraphs that fly in from the bottom of the slide, one by one, each time the presenter clicks with the mouse

Less is more. Animation can distract an audience, so use it sparingly.

Adding Animations

PowerPoint offers more than 40 animations you can add to objects on a slide by using a single command. For example, the Fade animation tells PowerPoint to gradually make objects on a slide fade into view after any transition effect is completed.

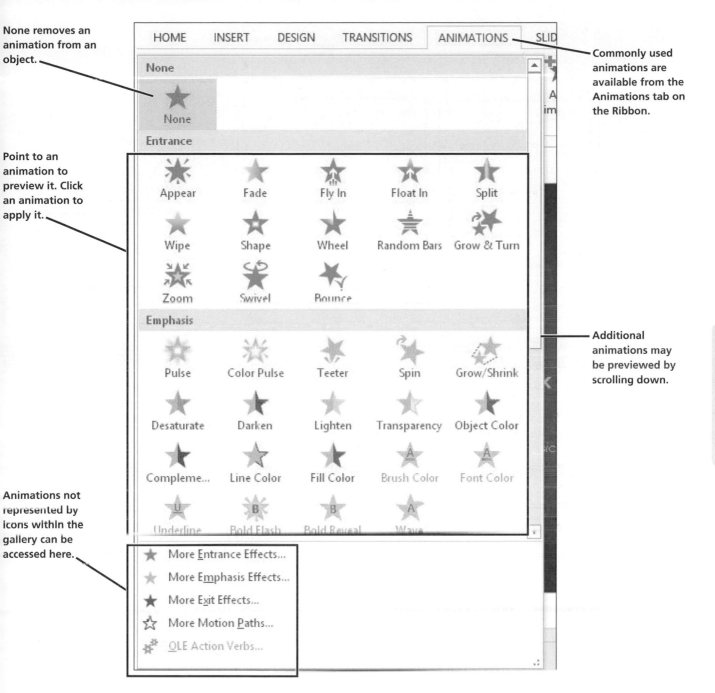

None removes an animation from an object.

Point to an animation to preview it. Click an animation to apply it.

Animations not represented by icons within the gallery can be accessed here.

Commonly used animations are available from the Animations tab on the Ribbon.

Additional animations may be previewed by scrolling down.

Setting Animation Options

After applying an animation to an object, you will likely want to set the animation options to control exactly how the animation effect works. The available options differ based on whether the animation was applied to text or an image. The options also differ based on the animation itself. Additionally, you can set timing options to control the speed of the animation.

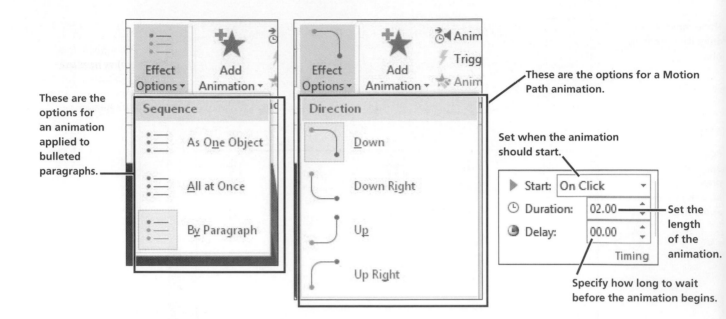

These are the options for an animation applied to bulleted paragraphs.

These are the options for a Motion Path animation.

Set when the animation should start.

Set the length of the animation.

Specify how long to wait before the animation begins.

QUICK REFERENCE	ADDING ANIMATION TO SLIDES
Task	**Procedure**
Apply a common animation to an object on a slide	■ Display the slide containing the object(s) to be animated. ■ Select the object (text object, picture, etc.) on the slide you wish to animate. ■ Choose Animations→Animation; choose the desired animation.
Set animation options	■ Select the object containing the animation. ■ Choose Animation→Animation→Effect Options menu ▼ and then choose the desired option. ■ Set the options in the Animation→Timing group if desired.
Remove an animation	■ Select the object containing the animation. ■ Choose Animation→Animation→None.

DEVELOP YOUR SKILLS PP03-D09

Apply Animation to Bulleted Paragraphs

In this exercise, you will apply an animation to text objects on a slide to draw attention to them.

1. Save your file as **PP03-D09-Animation-[FirstInitialLastName]**.

2. Choose **View→Presentation Views→Normal** 🔲.

3. Display the **Our Services** slide.

4. Click once in the **bulleted text** so a dashed border appears around the text box.

5. Choose **Animations→Animation→More→Entrance→Float In**.
   The animation previews, and you see each first-level paragraph animate across the slide.

6. Choose **Animations→Animation→Effect Option→Float Down** to have the paragraphs animate from the top of the slide down.

The numbers next to each bulleted paragraph indicate the order in which the animation is applied. By default, each paragraph will animate after a mouse click.

7. Choose **Slide Show→Start Slide Show→From Beginning** to start the slide show.

8. Click anywhere with the mouse to advance to the second slide.

The transition effect animates, but no bulleted paragraph appears yet.

9. Click anywhere with the mouse.

The first bulleted paragraph animates into view.

10. Continue clicking until all four bulleted paragraphs are visible and the slide show advances to the third slide, Our Recent Success.

11. Tap Esc to end the slide show and return to Normal view.

12. Save your presentation.

Using the Animation Pane

Video Library   http://labyrinthelab.com/videos   Video Number: PP13-V0311

By using the Animation pane, you have many more choices for effects than you have in the animation menu you used previously. You can also individually set the animation for each element on a slide. When using the Animation pane, you can control the visual effects, timing, and sequencing of the animation process. For example, rather than having to click each time to display the next animated bulleted paragraph, you can set it so that the animation starts automatically after the slide transition and continues until all objects on the slide have been animated.

Budgeting Your Time

Using the Animation pane to customize each animation is a time-consuming process. Be prepared to spend a significant amount of time selecting each animated object individually and then setting its options. The following figure describes the options on the Animation pane.

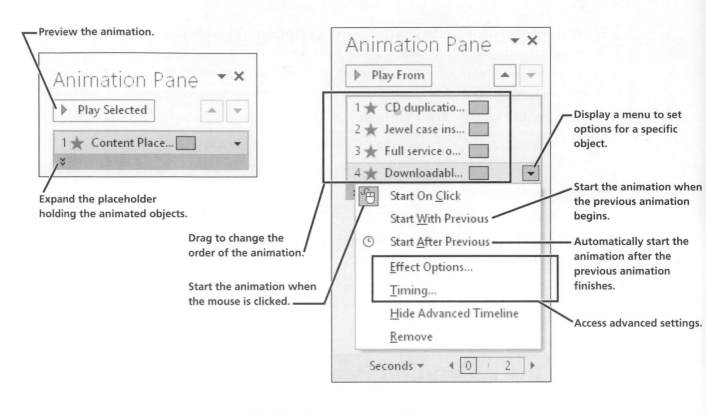

Preview the animation.

Expand the placeholder holding the animated objects.

Drag to change the order of the animation.

Start the animation when the mouse is clicked.

Display a menu to set options for a specific object.

Start the animation when the previous animation begins.

Automatically start the animation after the previous animation finishes.

Access advanced settings.

Use the Animation Pane

In this exercise, you will use the Animation pane to configure the bulleted paragraphs to animate automatically after the slide transition completes. This reduces the need for you to click constantly during a slide show.

1. Save your file as **PP03-D10-Animation-[FirstInitialLastName]**.

2. Display the second slide, **Our Services**.

3. Click once in the bulleted text so a dashed border appears around the text box.

4. Choose **Animations→Advanced Animation→Animation Pane**.

   The Animation pane displays on the right side of the screen.

5. Follow these steps to begin to configure the advanced animation settings:

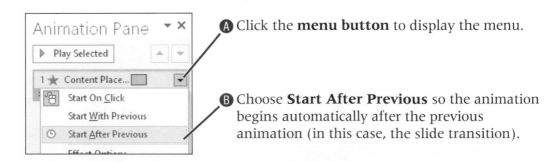

Ⓐ Click the **menu button** to display the menu.

Ⓑ Choose **Start After Previous** so the animation begins automatically after the previous animation (in this case, the slide transition).

Notice that the numbers next to each bulleted paragraph in the Animation panel have changed to zeros, indicating their animations all happen at the same time, automatically, after the slide transition.

6. Click the **Click to Expand Contents** bar to show each individual paragraph.

7. Follow these steps to customize the animation for the last paragraph:

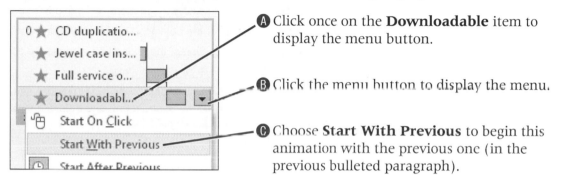

Ⓐ Click once on the **Downloadable** item to display the menu button.

Ⓑ Click the menu button to display the menu.

Ⓒ Choose **Start With Previous** to begin this animation with the previous one (in the previous bulleted paragraph).

8. Choose **Slide Show→Start Slide Show→From Beginning**.

9. Click anywhere with the mouse to advance to the second slide.

    The bulleted paragraphs animate automatically after the slide transition ends. Each animation happens sequentially, except for the last bulleted paragraph, which animates with the previous item.

10. Tap ⌜Esc⌝ to end the slide show and return to Normal view.

11. Save your presentation.

Adding Sound Effects

Video Library   http://labyrinthelab.com/videos   Video Number: PP13-V0312

PowerPoint 2013 provides audio clips and sound effects to accompany or accentuate your slide elements. For example, you may attach sound effects to slide transitions or animations. You can use the Transitions tab to add a sound to a slide transition or the Animation pane to add a sound to an animation.

| TRANSITIONS | ANIMATIONS | SLIDE SHOW | REVIEW | VIEW |

... itch   Flip   Gallery   Cube   Effect Options ▾   🔊 Sound: Applause   ⏱ Duration: 02.00   ⧉ Apply To All

Transition to This Slide   Timing

— An example of a sound effect added to a slide transition

Adding a Sound Effect to an Animation

Sometimes you don't want a sound effect to play during a slide transition, but rather when an animation causes an object to move across the slide. The following table describes the steps used to apply sound effects to animations.

QUICK REFERENCE	ADDING SOUND TO SLIDES
Task	**Procedure**
Add sound to an animation	■ Display the slide with the animation to which you wish to add sound (or add an animation to the slide object).
	■ Choose Animations→Advanced Animation→Animation Pane.
	■ Click the menu button for the object to receive sound and choose Effect Options.
	■ In the Enhancements section of the dialog box, choose the sound you wish to apply; click OK.
Add sound to a transition	■ Select a slide from the Slides panel or Slide Sorter view.
	■ Choose Transitions→Timing→Sound menu and then select a sound effect. The sound will play as the selected slide loads.

DEVELOP YOUR SKILLS PP03-D11

Apply Sound Effects

In this exercise, you will apply two sounds to the presentation to enhance an animation.

1. Save your file as **PP03-D11-Animation-[FirstInitialLastName]**.

2. Choose the **Our Recent Success** slide and then select the clip art object.

3. Choose **Animations→Animation→More→Entrance→Bounce**.

4. Click the drop-down menu for the clip art animation in the Animation pane and choose **Effect Options**.

5. Click the **Sound drop-down menu** in the Effect tab and choose the **Applause** sound effect.

6. Click **OK**, and the animation and sound will be previewed.

Apply a Transition Sound Effect

7. Display the **Our Services** slide.

8. Follow these steps to add a transition sound effect:

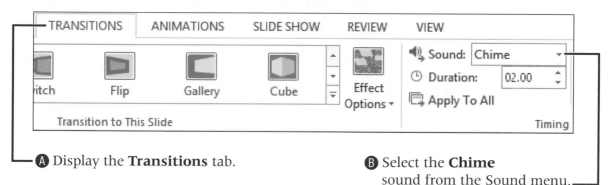

Ⓐ Display the **Transitions** tab.

Ⓑ Select the **Chime** sound from the Sound menu.

PowerPoint applies the Chime sound to the transition effect for this slide.

9. Choose **Slide Show→Start Slide Show→From Beginning** 🖥.

10. Navigate through the presentation until you hear the applause and see the Bounce animation on the Our Recent Success slide.

You may not be able to hear the sound effect if your computer does not have speakers.

11. Press the [Esc] key to end the slide show early and return to Normal view.

12. Close the **Animation pane**.

13. Save your presentation and exit **PowerPoint**.

Concepts Review

To check your knowledge of the key concepts introduced in this lesson, complete the Concepts Review quiz by choosing the appropriate access option below.

If you are...	Then access the quiz by...
Using the Labyrinth Video Library	Going to http://labyrinthelab.com/videos
Using eLab	Logging in, choosing Content, and navigating to the Concepts Review quiz for this lesson
Not using the Labyrinth Video Library or eLab	Going to the student resource center for this book

Reinforce Your Skills

Work with Images

In this exercise, you will add clip art to the Kids for Change animation presentation to add visual interest.

Prepare a Slide for ClipArt

1. Start **PowerPoint**. Open **PP03-R01-KidsClipArt** from the **PP2013 Lesson 03** folder and save it as `PP03-R01-KidsClipArt-[FirstInitialLastName]`.

2. Choose the **Events** slide (the second slide).

3. Choose **Home→Slides→Layout→Two Content**.

Insert ClipArt

4. Click the **Online Pictures** icon on the slide to display the Insert Pictures search window.

5. Type `calendar` in the Office.com search box and tap Enter.

6. Scroll through the results until you find an appropriate image.

7. Choose a clip art image that appeals to you and click **Insert**.

Move and Size Clip Art

8. Drag any of the image's corner handles to resize it so it fills the right half of the slide.

9. Drag from the center of the image to move and position it so it does not overlap any text.

10. Drag the rotate handle above the top edge of the image to rotate it slightly for visual interest.

Format Clip Art

11. Locate the **Picture Tools→Format→Picture Styles** group of commands.

12. Point to several of the thumbnail samples in the **Picture Styles gallery** to preview them and then click one to apply it. Choose a style that works well with your image. The following figure shows the **Reflected Rounded Rectangle** style applied.

Remove a Background

13. Display the **Contact Us** slide.

14. Choose **Insert→Images→Pictures**.

15. Browse to your **PP2013 Lesson 03** folder and insert the **PP03-R01-Phone** image.

16. With the phone image selected on the slide, choose **Picture Tools→Format→ Adjust→Remove Background**.

17. Drag the handles of the Background Removal border so the phone and wire are inside the border and then choose **Background Removal→Close→Keep Changes**.

Apply Artistic Effects

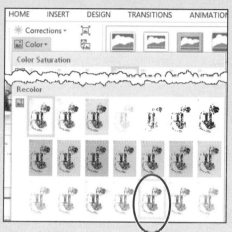

18. With the phone image selected on the slide, choose **Picture Tools→Format→Adjust→ Artistic Effects→Pencil Sketch**.

19. Choose **Picture Tools→Format→Adjust→Color →Recolor→Dark Green, Accent Color 4 Light**.

20. Move the phone, if necessary, so it is roughly centered below the phone number.

21. Save the changes and then exit **PowerPoint**. Submit your final file based on the guidelines provided by your instructor.

To view examples of how your file or files should look at the end of this exercise, go to the student resource center.

Add Shapes and Animations

In this exercise, you will create a custom shape of a house and incorporate animation to add visual appeal to the presentation.

Add and Resize a Shape

1. Start **PowerPoint**. Open **PP03-R02-KidsAnimated** from the **PP2013 Lesson 03** folder and save it as PP03-R02-KidsAnimated-[FirstInitialLastName].

2. Display the second slide, **This Month**.

3. Choose **Insert→Illustrations→Shapes→Rectangles→Rectangle**.

4. Drag on the slide to draw a rectangle. Resize and move it so it roughly matches this figure.

5. Choose **Insert→Illustrations→Shapes→Basic Shapes→Isosceles Triangle**.

6. Drag on the slide to draw a triangle to act as the roof of the house. Resize and move it so it roughly matches the figure in step 8.

7. Choose **Insert→Illustrations→Shapes→Rectangles→Rectangle**.

8. Drag on the slide to draw a small rectangle to act as a chimney. Resize and move it so it roughly matches this figure.

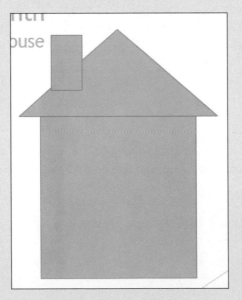

Merge Shapes

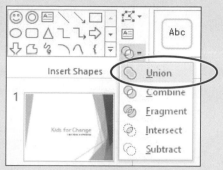

9. Click the large rectangle on the slide to select it, [Shift] + click the triangular roof, and [Shift] + click the small chimney so that all three shapes are selected.

10. Choose **Drawing Tools→Format→Insert Shapes→Merge Shapes→Union**.

11. Choose **Insert→Illustrations→Shapes→Rectangles →Rectangle**.

12. Drag on the slide to draw a rectangle to act as the door. Resize and move it so it roughly matches this figure.

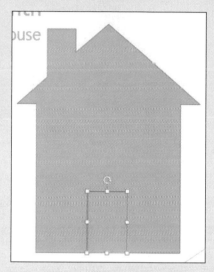

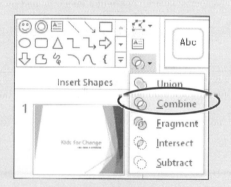

13. Click the door shape to select it, if necessary, and then [Shift] +click the house so both shapes are selected.

14. Choose **Drawing Tools→Format→Insert Shapes→Merge Shapes→Combine**.

Format and Add Text to a Shape

15. Click the dashed border of the shape to select it.

16. Type **Home** [Enter] **Sweet** [Enter] **Home** [Enter].

17. Click the dashed border of the shape to select it.

18. Choose **Home→Font→Font Size→36**. If your text no longer fits in the shape, choose a smaller font size or adjust the size of the house shape.

19. Choose **Drawing Tools→Format→Shape Styles→More→Intense Effect – Blue, Accent 2** (the bottom thumbnail in the third column).

20. Resize and move the shape so it fits in the upper-right area of the slide. You may have to adjust the font size.

Apply Transition Effects

21. Select slide 2, **This Month**, in the Slides panel.

22. ⌷Shift⌷ +click the last slide in the Slides panel so all but the title slide are selected.

23. Choose **Transitions→Transition to This Slide→More→Random Bars**.

Add Animation

24. Display the second slide, **This Month**, if necessary.

25. Click the house shape to select it.

26. Choose **Animations→Animation→More→Entrance→Bounce**.

27. Choose **Animations→Timing→Start→After Previous**.

28. Click the up arrow on the **Animations→Timing→Delay** box four times to set the delay to 1 second.

29. Display the third slide, **Event Benefits**.

30. Click in any text in the left column so a dashed border appears around the text box.

31. Choose **Animations→Animation→More→Entrance→Float In**.

32. Click in any of the text in the right column so a dashed border appears around the text box.

33. Choose **Animations→Animation→More→Entrance→Float In**.

34. Choose **Animations→Advanced Animation→Animation Pane**.

35. Click the arrows to expand the top group of content in the Animation pane.

36. Click the second item, **Homeless families**, to display its menu button.

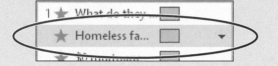

37. Click the item's menu button and then choose **Start After Previous**.

38. Click the third item, **$0 mortgage**, to display its menu button.

39. Click the item's menu button and then choose **Start After Previous**.

40. Click the fourth item, **A fresh start**, to display its menu button.

41. Click the item's menu button and then choose **Start After Previous**.

42. Expand the contents of the second group of content and set each item in the second group to **Start After Previous**.

Add a Sound Effect to an Animation

43. Display the second slide, **This Month**.

44. Click the house shape to select it.

45. Click the single item in the Animation pane, click its menu button, and choose **Effect Options** to view the effect's options.

46. Set the **Sound** menu to **Whoosh** and then click **OK**.

47. Close the **Animation pane**.

48. Choose **Slide Show→Start Slide Show→From Beginning** and click each slide until the slide show ends and you return to Normal view.

49. Save the changes and then exit **PowerPoint**. Submit your final file based on the guidelines provided by your instructor.

To view examples of how your file or files should look at the end of this exercise, go to the student resource center.

Add Visual Interest

In this exercise, you will add images and animation to a presentation.

Prepare a Slide for ClipArt

1. Start **PowerPoint**. Open **PP03-R03-KidsVisual** from the **PP2013 Lesson 03** folder and save it as `PP03-R03-KidsVisual-[FirstInitialLastName]`.

2. Display the third slide.

3. Choose **Home→Slides→Layout→Two Content**.

Insert ClipArt

4. Click the **Pictures** icon on the slide to insert a picture from your computer.

5. Browse to your **PP2013 Lesson 03** folder and insert the **PP03-R03-Girl** picture.

6. Drag the picture to roughly fill the right side of the slide.

7. Display the fourth slide.

8. Choose **Home→Slides→Layout→Two Content**.

9. Click the **Pictures** icon on the slide to insert a picture from your computer.

10. Browse to your **PP2013 Lesson 03** folder and insert the **PP03-R03-Truck** picture.

11. Drag the truck picture to roughly center it on the slide.

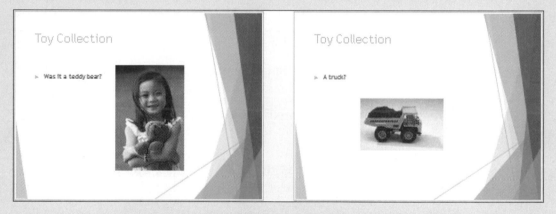

12. Display the fifth slide.

13. Choose **Insert→Images→Online Pictures**.

14. Type **toy** in the Office.com search box and tap Enter.

15. Scroll through the results until you find a toy you like, and then click the toy to select it.

16. Continue to scroll and look for more toys. Ctrl+click additional toys to add them to your selection. After you have selected a total of six toys, click **Insert**.

Move, Size, and Rotate ClipArt

17. Click an empty area of the slide to deselect the inserted pictures.

18. Click one of the toys on the slide to select it.

19. Drag a corner handle on the picture's border to make the picture smaller.

20. Drag the rotate handle above the top edge of the picture to slightly rotate it.

21. Drag the picture to move it to a position of your liking.

22. Resize, rotate, and move the remaining toys so your slide roughly matches the following figure. *Do not be concerned if the picture backgrounds overlap each other at this point.*

Format Clip Art

23. Display the third slide and click the picture of the girl and her teddy bear.

24. Choose **Picture Tools→Format →Picture Styles→More→Rotated, White**.

25. Drag the picture to reposition it, if necessary.

Remove a Background

26. Display slide 4 and click the truck picture.

27. Choose **Picture Tools→Format→Adjust→Remove Background**.

28. Drag the handles of the background removal border until the truck fits inside it.

29. Choose **Background Removal→Refine→Mark Areas to Remove**.

30. Drag on the light colored areas on the ground near the tires to remove them.

31. Choose **Background Removal→Close→Keep Changes**.

32. Drag a corner handle of the truck's border to resize it and then drag the truck into position so it roughly matches the following figure.

33. Display slide 5 and remove the background of the pictures so they can be overlapped.

Apply Artistic Effects

34. Display slide 3 and click the picture of the girl.

35. Choose **Picture Tools→Format→Adjust→Artistic Effects→Glow, Diffused**.

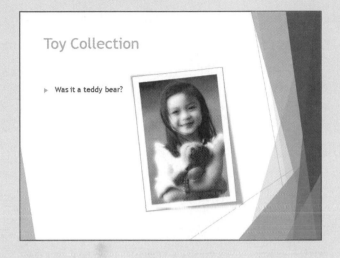

Add and Format a Shape with Text

36. Choose **Insert→Illustrations→Shapes→Stars and Banners→Up Ribbon**.

37. ⌈Shift⌉+drag to create a proportional ribbon that fills the left side of the slide under the text.

38. Type **My 1st toy**.

39. Click the blue ribbon shape to select it.

40. Tap ⌈Ctrl⌉+⌈C⌉ to copy the shape.

41. Display the fourth slide with the truck.

42. Tap ⌈Ctrl⌉+⌈V⌉ to paste the shape.

43. Drag the truck picture so the blue ribbon doesn't overlap it.

44. Click the blue ribbon shape to select it.

45. Choose **Drawing Tools→Format→Shape Styles→Shape Effects→Reflection→Reflection Variations→Half Reflection, Touching**.

46. Choose **Home→Clipboard→Format Painter** to copy the formatting.

47. Display the third slide and click the blue ribbon to duplicate the shape's effect.

Apply Transition Effects

48. Choose **View→Presentation Views→Slide Sorter**.

49. Click slide 2 and then Shift+click slide 5 so that all but the title slide are selected.

50. Choose **Transitions→Transition to This Slide→More→Exciting→Vortex**.

51. Choose **Transitions→Transition to This Slide→Effect Options→From Top**.

52. Click the down arrow of the **Transitions→Timing→Duration** box until the Duration is set to **02.00**.

Apply Animation

53. Double-click slide 5 to display it in **Normal** view.

54. Click one of the toys on the slide to select it.

55. Choose **Animations→Animation→More→Entrance→Grow & Turn**.

56. Click a second toy on the slide to select it.

57. Choose **Animations→Animation→More→Entrance→Grow & Turn**.

58. One at a time, click each remaining toy and apply the **Grow & Turn** animation.

Use the Animation Pane

59. Choose **Animations→Advanced Animation→Animation Pane**.

60. Click the first animated item in the Animation pane to display its menu button.

61. Click the menu button and choose **Start After Previous**.

62. One at a time, click each remaining item and set them to **Start After Previous**.

Add a Sound Effect to an Animation

63. Click the last item in the Animation pane, click its menu button, and choose **Effect Options**.

64. Set the sound effect to **Applause** and then click **OK**.

65. Close the **Animation** pane.

66. Choose **Slide Show→Start Slide Show→From Beginning** and click each slide to view the presentation, returning to **Normal** view when you are finished.

67. Save the changes and then exit **PowerPoint**. Submit your final file based on the guidelines provided by your instructor.

Apply Your Skills

Work with Images

In this exercise, you will add pictures and remove the backgrounds for the Universal Corporate Events presentation. You will also format the pictures to enhance the visual appeal of the slides.

Prepare a Slide for and Insert Clip Art

1. Start **PowerPoint**. Open **PP03-A01-UniversalClipArt** from the **PP2013 Lesson 03** folder and save it as **PP03-A01-UniversalClipArt-[FirstInitialLastName]**.

2. Choose the **Catering** slide (the third slide).

3. Apply the **Two Content** layout.

4. Apply the **Two Content** layout to slides 4–9.

5. Display slide 3.

6. Click the **Online Pictures** icon on the slide to display the Insert Pictures search window.

7. Search for and insert a photo appropriate for a catering slide.

8. Search for and insert an appropriate photograph on slides 4–9. The photograph should represent the slide's text content.

Move, Size, and Rotate Objects

9. Resize and reposition the photographs on each slide so they fill the right half of the slide.

Format Clip Art

10. Add a **Picture Style** or **Picture Effect** to each photograph. Use a maximum of two styles of effects.

Remove a Background and Apply Artistic Effects

11. Remove the backgrounds of each photo. You may want to resize or move the photos after removing the background.

12. Display slide 5, **Graphic Design**, and apply an **Artistic Effect** to the photo.

13. Save the changes and then exit **PowerPoint**. Submit your final file based on the guidelines provided by your instructor.

    To view examples of how your file or files should look at the end of this exercise, go to the student resource center.

Add Shapes and Animations

In this exercise, you will add shapes and animation to a presentation.

Add and Resize a Shape with Text

1. Start **PowerPoint**. Open **PP03-A02-UniversalAnimated** from the **PP2013 Lesson 03** folder and save it as **PP03-A02-UniversalAnimated-[FirstInitialLastName]**.

2. Display the third slide, **Vegan**.

3. Insert the **Explosion 1** shape.

4. Type **Certified Vegan!**

5. Resize and reposition the shape so it fills the area below the text.

6. Enlarge the font size of the shape's text to be as large as possible while remaining inside the shape.

7. Add the **Explosion 2** shape to slide 4 with the text **Certified Kosher!**

8. Resize and reposition the **shape** so it fills the area below the text.

9. Enlarge the font size of the shape's text to be as large as possible while remaining inside the shape.

10. Add the **Up Ribbon** shape to slide 5 with the text **Certified Organic!**

11. Resize and reposition the shape so it fills the area below the text.

12. Enlarge the font size of the shape's text to be as large as possible while remaining inside the shape.

Merge and Format Shapes

13. Display the last slide.

14. Insert a **Rectangle** shape and resize it so it is tall and thin.

15. Insert a **Teardrop** shape and adjust the size and shape so it looks like a candle flame. Position it on top of the thin rectangle.

16. Merge the **Rectangle** and **Teardrop** shapes into a single candle shape.

17. Copy the new candle shape and paste three copies on the slide, arranging them similarly to the following figure.

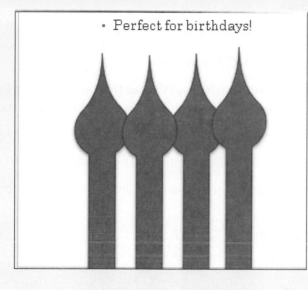

18. Apply the **Intense Effect – Blue-Gray, Accent 2** Shape Style to the shapes on slides 3–6.

Apply Transition Effects and Animations

19. Select all slides but the title slide.

20. Apply the **Checkerboard** transition and set the **Effect Options** to **From Top**.

21. Display the second slide, **Catering**.

22. Apply the **Fade** animation to the bulleted paragraphs.

23. Use the Animation pane to select the Kosher Dishes item and set it to **Start With Previous**.

24. Set *Meat-lovers dishes* and *Desserts* to **Start With Previous** so that all four paragraphs will fade in at the same time after a click.

Add a Sound Effect to an Animation

25. Select the *Vegan dishes* item in the Animation pane and apply the **Applause** sound effect.

26. Close the **Animation pane**.

27. Choose **Slide Show→Start Slide Show→From Beginning** and click each slide until the slide show ends and you return to Normal view.

28. Save the changes and then exit **PowerPoint**. Submit your final file based on the guidelines provided by your instructor.

To view examples of how your file or files should look at the end of this exercise, go to the student resource center.

Add Visual Interest

In this exercise, you will add images and animation to a presentation.

Prepare a Slide for and Insert Clip Art

1. Start **PowerPoint**. Open **PP03-A03-UniversalVisual** from the **PP2013 Lesson 03** folder and save it as **PP03-A03-UniversalVisual-[FirstInitialLastName]**.

2. Display the second slide and change its layout to **Two Content**.

3. Use the **Online Pictures** icon on the slide to search **Office.com** and insert a photo of a bus.

4. Use the **Ribbon** to search **Office.com** for a photo of a limousine and another photo of a ferry boat, and then insert them.

Move, Size, Rotate, and Format Clip Art

5. Resize and position the three images on the slide to your liking.

6. Apply a **Picture Style** to each of the pictures. Use the same style on all three pictures to maintain consistency.

Remove a Background and Apply Artistic Effects

7. Display the title slide.

8. Insert the **PPT03-A03-Hand** picture from the **PP2013 Lesson 03** folder.

9. Use the **Background Removal** tool to remove the white background of the picture.

10. Move the picture to the lower-right corner of the slide.

11. Apply the **Photocopy** artistic effect to the picture.

12. Adjust the **Color** of the picture to a **Color Tone** of **Temperature: 7200k**.

Add, Merge, and Format Shapes

13. On the third slide, draw a wide **Rounded Rectangle**, a small **Rounded Rectangle**, and two **Circles** and then arrange them into the shape of a bus.

14. Merge the shapes into a single bus shape.

15. On the fourth slide, use the **Rectangle**, **Oval**, **Right Triangle**, and **Manual Operation** shapes to create a limousine. (The Manual Operation shape is in the Flowchart category.)

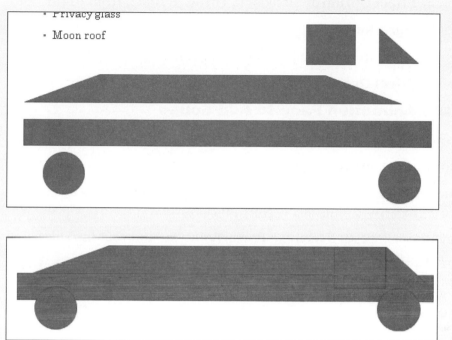

16. Merge the shapes into a single shape.

17. On the fifth slide, use the **Rectangle** and **Manual Operation** shapes to create a ferry boat.

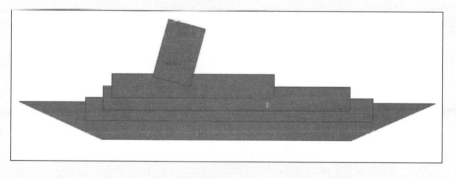

18. Merge the shapes into a single shape.

19. Apply the **Intense Effect – Olive Green, Accent 3** Shape Style to each of the shapes on slides 3–5.

20. Resize and position the shapes so they fill the maximum area of their slides without overlapping the text.

Apply Transition Effects and Add Animation

21. Apply the **Reveal** transition to all but the title slide.

22. Set the **Effect Option** on all slides to **Through Black from Right**.

23. Set the **Duration** on all slides to **3 seconds**.

24. Apply the **Fly In** animation to the hand picture on the title slide.

25. Set the **Effect Option** to **From Right**.

Use the Animation Pane to Add Sound

26. Use the **Animation Pane** to add the **Whoosh** sound effect to the hand's animation.

27. Close the **Animation** pane.

28. Choose **Slide Show→Start Slide Show→From Beginning** and click each slide to view the presentation, returning to **Normal** view when you are finished.

29. Save the changes and then exit **PowerPoint**. Submit your final file based on the guidelines provided by your instructor.

Extend Your Skills

In the course of working through the Extend Your Skills exercises, you will think critically as you use the skills taught in the lesson to complete the assigned projects. To evaluate your mastery and completion of the exercises, your instructor may use a rubric, with which more points are allotted according to performance characteristics. (The more you do, the more you earn!) Ask your instructor how your work will be evaluated.

PP03-E01 That's the Way I See It

New PowerPoint users often overuse transitions, animation, and sound effects. In this exercise, you will see how sometimes less is more. Create a presentation with at least six slides. Every slide except the title slide should include a title, text, and an image. Apply any design theme and variation. Make sure the presentation focuses on a single idea (for example, a classic car collection, your favorite movies, or inspirational people). Apply a different transition to each slide. Apply a different animation to each text block and each image. Add a different sound effect to each slide. In other words—overdo it! Save your file as **PP03-E01-AnimationOverkill-[FirstInitialLastName]** in the **PP2013 Lesson 03** folder. View the presentation as a slide show.

Save a copy of the presentation as **PP03-E01-AnimationAppropriate-[FirstInitialLastName]**. Edit the presentation so that each slide uses the same subtle transition. Remove the animation from each image, and standardize the animation on the text blocks. Choose a subtle Entrance animation. Remove all sound effects. Save your changes. View the revised presentation as a slide show and compare it to your "overkill" version.

You will be evaluated based on the inclusion of all elements specified, your ability to follow directions, your ability to apply newly learned skills to a real-world situation, your creativity, and the relevance of your topic and/or data choice(s). Submit your final files based on the guidelines provided by your instructor.

PP03-E02 Be Your Own Boss

In this exercise, you will edit the animation on the Blue Jean Landscaping presentation. Open **PP03-E02-BlueJeanAnimated** from the **PP2013 Lesson 03** folder and save it as **PP03-E02-BlueJeanAnimated-[FirstInitialLastName]**. View the presentation as a slide show and notice where the animations occur. Edit the presentation so the animations occur when a slide is clicked rather than automatically. Also, make sure the bulleted text animates one line at a time. Add a final slide using the Section Header layout. Use the title **Get Outside More** and the subtitle **It'll do you good!**. Insert **PPT03-E02-Flowers** from the **PP2013 Lesson 03** folder. Make these changes:

- Remove the photo background.
- Move the image to appear behind the text.
- Apply an adjustment to make it less distracting.
- Apply the same slide transition used by the other slides.
- Add a sound effect that you feel is appropriate.

You will be evaluated based on the inclusion of all elements specified, your ability to follow directions, your ability to apply newly learned skills to a real-world situation, your creativity, and your demonstration of an entrepreneurial spirit. Submit your final file based on the guidelines provided by your instructor.

Transfer Your Skills

In the course of working through the Transfer Your Skills exercises, you will use critical-thinking and creativity skills to complete the assigned projects using skills taught in the lesson. To evaluate your mastery and completion of the exercises, your instructor may use a rubric, with which more points are allotted according to performance characteristics. (The more you do, the more you earn!) Ask your instructor how your work will be evaluated.

PP03-T01 Use the Web as a Learning Tool

Throughout this book, you will be provided with an opportunity to use the Internet as a learning tool by completing WebQuests. According to the original creators of WebQuests, as described on their website (WebQuest.org), a WebQuest is "an inquiry-oriented activity in which most or all of the information used by learners is drawn from the web." To complete the WebQuest projects in this book, navigate to the student resource center and choose the WebQuest for the lesson on which you are currently working. The subject of each WebQuest will be relevant to the material found in the lesson.

WebQuest Subject: Licensing Media Usage

Submit your final file(s) based on the guidelines provided by your instructor.

PP03-T02 Demonstrate Proficiency

Stormy BBQ needs a slideshow to play on television screens throughout their seating area. It should feature images of mouth-watering barbeque. Create a PowerPoint presentation with at least five slides. Each slide should display a single photo of delicious barbeque. Remove the backgrounds from the images you use, as necessary. Use slide transitions to fade one slide into the next. Include an animated title on each slide that names the dish.

Choose one slide on which to add a shape. Add a shape from the Stars and Banners category with the text **Blue Ribbon Winner**. Format the shape and its text to add visual interest while keeping the text easy to read.

Save the presentation as **PP03-T02-BBQSlideShow-[FirstInitialLastName]** in your **PP2013 Lesson 03** folder.

Submit your final file based on the guidelines provided by your instructor.

Inserting Charts

LEARNING OBJECTIVES

After studying this lesson, you will be able to:

- Insert charts to display numerical data
- Link to and use data in an Excel spreadsheet to create a chart
- Format charts and change chart types
- Repair broken links to external documents
- Create SmartArt diagrams

A cornerstone of the Microsoft Office suite of programs is the seamless way programs join, or integrate with each other. For example, in this lesson, you will learn how to place an Excel workbook into a PowerPoint presentation to harness the strength of Excel features in PowerPoint. You will also take advantage of the Microsoft Graph charting program to create dynamic and precise charts in your presentation. Finally, you will use SmartArt to add a beautifully arranged organization chart that is clear, concise, and stylish.

Adding Charts to Presentations

You continue to develop PowerPoint presentations for iJams, deciding it is time to expand iJams by opening a recording studio that local musicians can rent to record their original music. You schedule a meeting with the loan committee at Twilight Hollow Bank. You are concerned that you will have to re-create your best Excel workbook of financial projections until you remember that you can simply link the Excel file to the PowerPoint presentation.

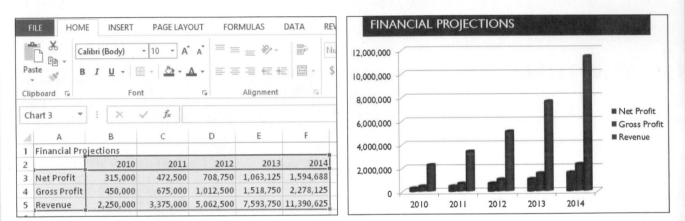

Inserting Charts

Video Library   http://labyrinthelab.com/videos   Video Number: PP13-V0401

PowerPoint is an intensely visual application. Although it is often the case that you will be creating presentations that represent concepts or goals, you may also present financial statistics or numerical data. PowerPoint allows you to create charts based on numerical data in a spreadsheet. If Microsoft Excel is installed, PowerPoint and Excel will work together to provide you with advanced options to design the chart layout and edit chart data. Without Excel installed, PowerPoint will use Microsoft Graph to create a new chart. Excel offers the more intuitive Ribbon interface, provides more formatting options, and creates more visually appealing charts than Microsoft Graph. Therefore, it is recommended that you use Excel to create charts for your PowerPoint presentations. In fact, if Excel is installed, PowerPoint launches it automatically whenever you insert a new chart.

Creating Embedded Charts

PowerPoint has four layouts (Title and Content, Two Content, Comparison, and Content with Caption) that make inserting new charts simple. Each of these common layouts includes an Insert Chart icon that you can click to insert a new chart. What if your slide doesn't use one of these layouts? You can always insert a chart manually from the Ribbon, no matter what layout your slide uses.

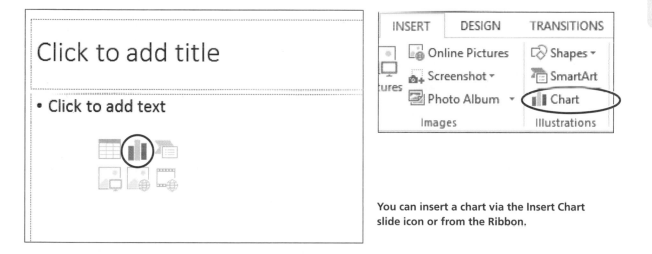

You can insert a chart via the Insert Chart slide icon or from the Ribbon.

Microsoft Graph

If Excel is not installed, PowerPoint launches a Microsoft Graph datasheet when you insert a new chart. (Microsoft Graph is a small program installed with many Office applications.) Charts created in Microsoft Graph lack the Chart Tools contextual Ribbon tabs and commands that are available with an Excel-generated chart for advanced formatting and easy editing (these tabs are discussed later in this lesson). A Microsoft Graph chart can be converted to Office 2013 format, which results in the contextual Ribbon tabs being made available and chart data editing handled by Excel. However, without Excel installed, a converted chart is not editable. The rest of this lesson assumes that you have Excel installed.

TIP

To convert a Microsoft Graph chart to Office 2013 format, double-click the chart on the slide and choose Convert. However, remember that Excel must be installed to edit numeric data in a converted chart.

Microsoft Graph datasheet

		A	B	C	D	E
		1st Qtr	2nd Qtr	3rd Qtr	4th Qtr	
1	East	20.4	27.4	90	20.4	
2	West	30.6	38.6	34.6	31.6	
3	North	45.9	46.9	45	43.9	
4						

Presentation1 - Datasheet

Excel spreadsheet

	A	B	C	D
1		Series 1	Series 2	Series 3
2	Category 1	4.3	2.4	2
3	Category 2	2.5	4.4	2
4	Category 3	3.5	1.8	3
5	Category 4	4.5	2.8	5

When you insert a new chart, PowerPoint starts you out with generic data labels and numbers that you replace with your own.

Choosing a Chart Type

Certain chart types are best suited to display specific types of data. Some of the most commonly used chart types are described in the following table.

Chart Type	Icon	Best Used to...
Column	Column	Show one-time (nonadjacent) results, such as those of a survey, depicted as vertical bars
Bar	Bar	Show the same type of results as a column chart, but with horizontal bars
Line	Line	Show continual change over time, such as profit / loss over several months
Pie	Pie	Compare a portion or portions to a whole, such as hours spent on various tasks in a single day

Editing Chart Data

When you create a new chart, PowerPoint launches a minimal version of Excel called Chart. A button at the top of the Chart window opens the full version of Excel. This way, you can edit data in a simple interface (Chart), or edit the data directly in Excel and take advantage of Excel's powerful tools for working with numeric data. Don't be confused when you insert a new chart and see data already entered in the spreadsheet window. This is sample data that PowerPoint inserts to get you started; simply replace it with your headings and numbers.

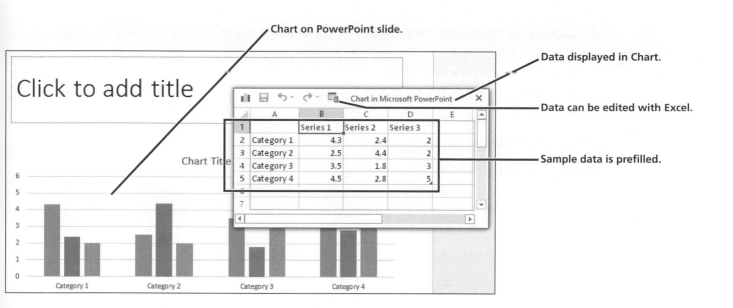

Chart on PowerPoint slide.

Data displayed in Chart.

Data can be edited with Excel.

Sample data is prefilled.

Formatting Charts

After a chart has been inserted, simply click the chart to select it. PowerPoint's Chart tools are displayed in the Ribbon as the Design and Format contextual tabs. You can use these tabs to create, modify, and format your chart without leaving the PowerPoint window.

Insert a Chart

In this exercise, you will create a chart inside your PowerPoint presentation and revise the default datasheet with your own custom data.

The instructions for this and other charting exercises assume that Excel 2013 is installed on your computer.

1. Start **PowerPoint**. Open **PP04-D01-Chart** from the **PP2013 Lesson 04** folder and save it as **PP04-D01-Chart-[FirstInitialLastName]**.

   Replace the bracketed text with your first initial and last name. For example, if your name is Bethany Smith, your filename would look like this: PP04-D01-Chart-BSmith.

2. Display slide 3, **Our Expansion Plan**.

   In the next few steps, you will add a new slide after Our Expansion Plan.

3. Choose **Home→Slides→New Slide** .

4. Choose **Home→Slides→ Layout →Two Content**.

   PowerPoint will apply the new layout, which includes a placeholder box on the left that you will use for your text, and a placeholder box on the right that you will use for your chart.

5. Type **Year-To-Date Results** as the title.

   The title is automatically formatted with all capitals because that is defined by the theme.

PowerPoint 2013

6. Click in the placeholder box on the left side and add the following bulleted text items, pressing ⌗Enter⌗ after each one except the last:

- **25% growth rate** ⌗Enter⌗
- **Positive cash flow** ⌗Enter⌗
- **Margins increasing**

Set Up the Chart

7. Click the **Insert Chart** ▮▮ icon in the middle of the placeholder box on the right side.

   The Insert Chart dialog box appears. Knowing the type of data you are charting will make it easier to select the appropriate type of chart. You are charting one-time results, so a column or bar graph is appropriate.

8. Follow these steps to insert a chart from the Insert Chart dialog box:

Ⓐ Choose the **Column** category.

Ⓑ Choose the **3-D Clustered Column** chart type.

Ⓒ Click **OK**.

The chart opens with sample data. You will replace the sample data with your own headings and numbers.

9. Follow these steps to set up the chart datasheet:

Ⓐ Click the cell with the text **Category 1**, type **Q1**, and tap ⌗Enter⌗.

Ⓑ Enter the **remaining data** shown here. Click a cell, type the cell data, and then click another cell.

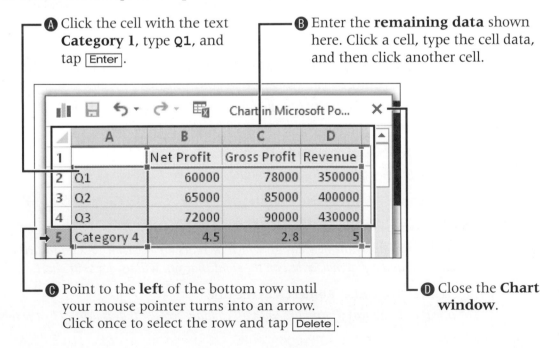

Ⓖ Point to the **left** of the bottom row until your mouse pointer turns into an arrow. Click once to select the row and tap ⌗Delete⌗.

Ⓓ Close the **Chart window**.

Your slide should now resemble the following illustration. Notice how tightly squeezed the chart appears. In the next topic, you will learn how to modify a chart to aid readability and make it visually attractive.

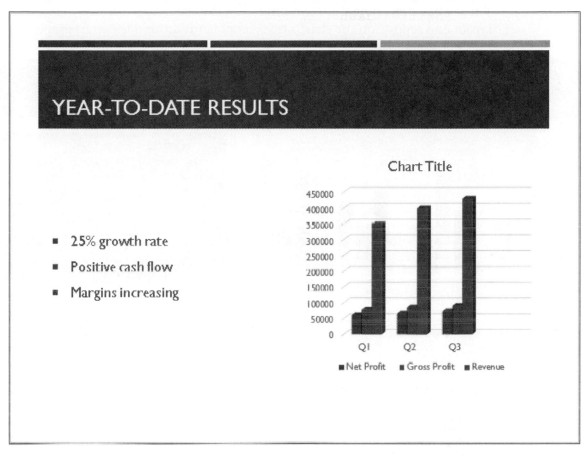

10. Save your presentation.

Modifying Charts

Video Library   http://labyrinthelab.com/videos   Video Number: PP13-V0402

After you insert a chart, you can make changes to it as necessary. For example, you can edit the chart data, change the color scheme, and even change to a different chart type. As you would expect, the two Chart Tools contextual tabs on the Ribbon give access to these modification commands.

 If you don't see the Chart Tools contextual tabs, make sure that the chart is selected (displays sizing handles).

Changing the Chart Size and Layout

You can size the chart by dragging the sizing handles, and you can position the chart by dragging it to a different location. These handles work just as they do on clip art and other figures on slides. You can also choose a different layout for the chart from the Design tab under Chart Tools.

Changing the Chart Type

Sometimes you may want to change the chart type to better display the data. For example, you might want to switch from a normal bar chart to a 3-D-style bar chart. Or you may want to use a stacked bar chart style if space is limited on the slide. Additionally, you can change the chart's layout and reposition the chart's text components around the chart graphic.

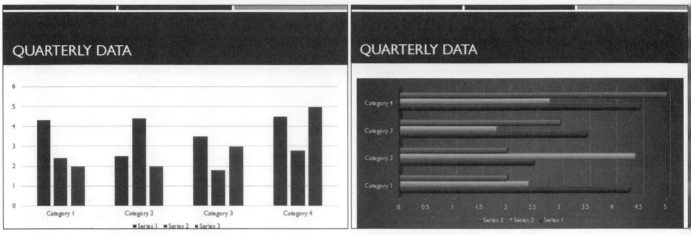

The same chart data first displayed as a Clustered Column, then as a 3-D Clustered Bar

QUICK REFERENCE	CHARTING IN POWERPOINT
Task	**Procedure**
Insert a chart	Click the Insert Chart icon on the slide or choose Insert→Illustrations→Chart.
Change the size of a chart	Point to a sizing handle around the chart's border. When the double-headed arrow appears, click and then drag the border.
Change the chart type	Select the chart and then choose Chart Tools→Design→Type→Change Chart Type.
Modify chart data	Select the chart and then choose Chart Tools→Design→Data→Edit Data.
Change the chart layout	Select the chart and then choose a layout from the Chart Tools→Design→Quick Layout gallery.

Modify a Chart

In this exercise, you will modify the chart slide by adjusting its size and editing the chart data.

1. Save your file as **PP04-D02-Chart-[FirstInitialLastName]**.

2. Follow these steps to resize the chart:

A If necessary, click anywhere in the chart to display its border.

B Point to the center of the left border until your mouse pointer becomes a double-arrow. Then, drag the border left until its left edge is just to the left of the letter *R* in *Results*.

C Use the same method to drag the right border until it snaps to the right edge of the slide.

D Use the same method to drag the bottom border until it snaps to the bottom edge of the slide.

You have resized the chart but have maintained some breathing room (white space) between the left border of the chart and the bulleted text. You have also maintained some white space between the right edge of the chart and the slide's right edge.

3. Make sure the chart is still selected and the Chart Tools contextual tabs are visible.

4. Choose **Chart Tools→Design→Data→Edit Data** 📊.

This is an embedded chart. You can always edit the data in an embedded chart by selecting this command.

5. Follow these steps to edit the chart:

Ⓐ Click in the **60000 cell**, type `160000`, and tap Enter.

Ⓑ Click the remaining **numerical cells** in **columns B and C** and increase them all by 100,000, tapping Enter after each change. The chart on the PowerPoint slide is updated every time you tap Enter.

Ⓒ Point to the bottom square handle of the data border until your pointer becomes a diagonal arrow. Then drag up one row to remove the empty row 5 from the data.

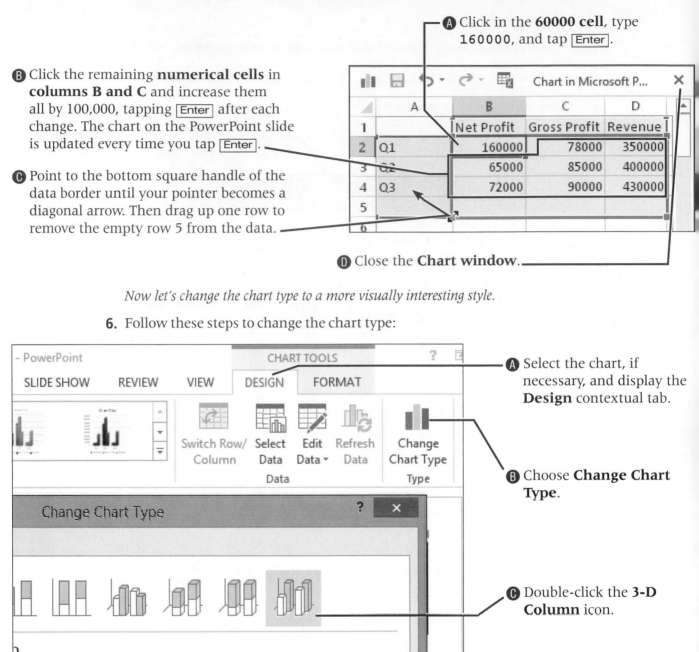

Ⓓ Close the **Chart window**.

Now let's change the chart type to a more visually interesting style.

6. Follow these steps to change the chart type:

Ⓐ Select the chart, if necessary, and display the **Design** contextual tab.

Ⓑ Choose **Change Chart Type**.

Ⓒ Double-click the **3-D Column** icon.

The chart type changes. However, the bars in the graph are too congested, and the text is difficult to read.

7. Choose **Chart Tools→Design→Chart Layouts→ Quick Layout→Layout 3**.

PowerPoint rearranges the slide layout to remove the text on the right side of the chart. The slide itself has a title, so we will delete the additional title inside the chart.

8. Click once on the **Chart Title** so it displays handles and then tap ⌐Delete⌐.

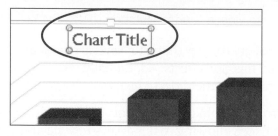

The chart title disappears. Your slide should resemble the following illustration.

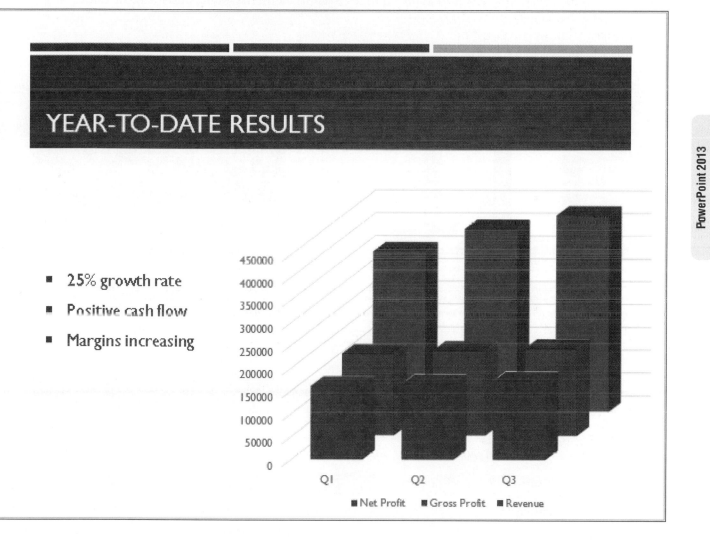

9. Save your presentation.

Changing Chart Style and Color Scheme

Video Library   http://labyrinthelab.com/videos   Video Number: PP13-V0403

You can format your charts with predesigned styles that alter several characteristics of the charts, including text used as labels, chart color fills, and effects. Additionally, you can change the colors used in a chart to make it stand out from the rest of the slide, or just make it easier to see from a distance.

While these changes can be made from the Ribbon, PowerPoint 2013 includes new chart buttons, which are also available in Excel, allowing easier access to style and color changes. PowerPoint charts now display three small buttons to the right of a selected chart, allowing you to quickly preview and apply changes to chart elements, style, and even the data being displayed.

Styles and colors can be changed here.

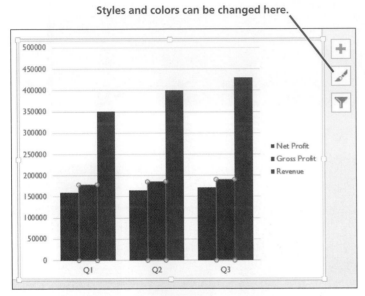

The default chart.

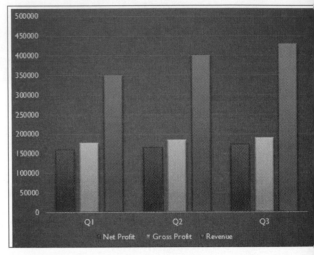

Chart after style and color are changed.

CHART BUTTONS		
Button Name	**Icon**	**What It Does**
Chart Elements	⊞	■ Show or hide chart title, axis labels, gridlines, and other chart elements.
		■ The same options are available from Chart Tools→Design→Chart Layouts→Add Chart Element.
Chart Styles	🖉	■ Change a chart style or color scheme.
		■ The same options are available from Chart Tools→Design→Chart Styles.
Chart Filter	▽	■ Filter chart data to display only desired data.

Style and Color a Chart

In this exercise, you will modify the chart elements, style, and color scheme by using the new chart buttons.

1. Save your file as **PP04-D03-Chart-[FirstInitialLastName]**.

2. Follow these steps to change the chart's style:

Ⓐ Select the chart, if necessary, to display the **chart buttons**.

Ⓑ Click the **Chart Styles** button.

Ⓒ Click **Style**.

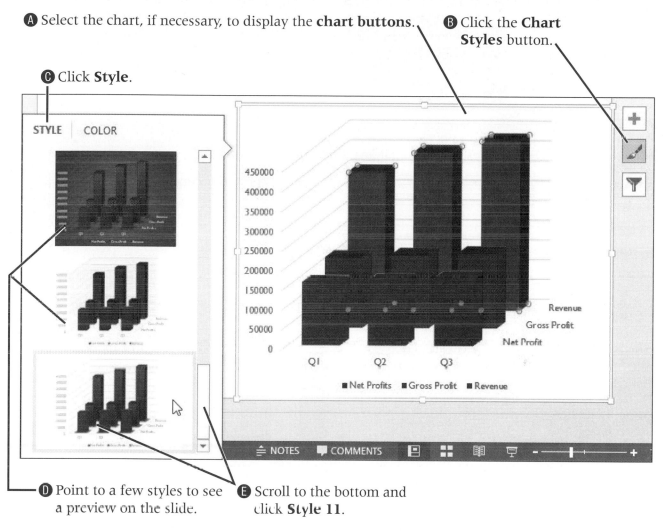

Ⓓ Point to a few styles to see a preview on the slide.

Ⓔ Scroll to the bottom and click **Style 11**.

The new style added back text to the right of the chart. You will delete it later in this exercise.

3. Follow these steps to change the chart's color scheme:

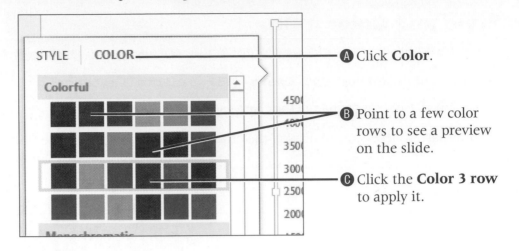

Ⓐ Click **Color**.

Ⓑ Point to a few color rows to see a preview on the slide.

Ⓒ Click the **Color 3 row** to apply it.

4. Follow these steps to change the chart's elements:

Ⓐ Click the **Chart Elements** button.

Ⓑ Point to each unchecked item to see a preview of the item on the chart. Do not click!

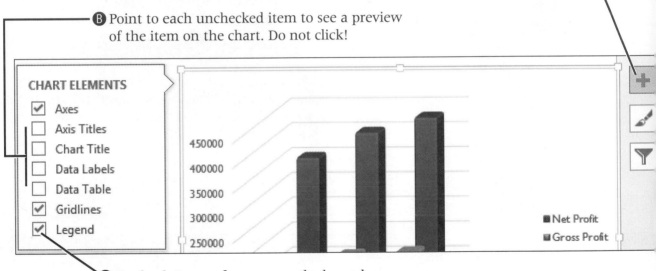

Ⓒ Uncheck **Legend** to remove the legend from the right side of the chart.

5. Click on the slide, but off the chart, to deselect it.

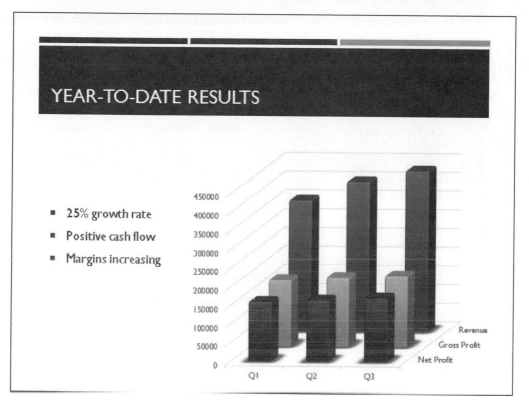

6. Save your presentation.

Working with External Excel Documents

Video Library   http://labyrinthelab.com/videos   Video Number: PP13-V0404

Office 2013 provides a variety of tools and techniques to let you exchange data between applications. Object Linking and Embedding (OLE) allows you to create links between source documents and destination documents. For example, you may want a chart in an existing Excel document to appear in a PowerPoint presentation. This makes it possible for another individual or department to maintain the Excel spreadsheet and its numerical data while you simply link to it and display an attractive chart based on its contents.

Benefits of Linking

Creating a chart in Excel and linking the chart object to PowerPoint gives you the opportunity to maintain modularity over presentation components. The Excel data remains in the Excel spreadsheet, which can be maintained by the financial wizards, while the PowerPoint presentation remains totally under your control as a separate document. Any changes made to the Excel document can be reflected in the chart displayed on the PowerPoint slide. Don't be worried if, during your actual presentation, the Excel spreadsheet is not available. The chart will still display beautifully. The Excel spreadsheet needs to be available only if you want to edit the chart data.

Changes to the Excel spreadsheet data here...

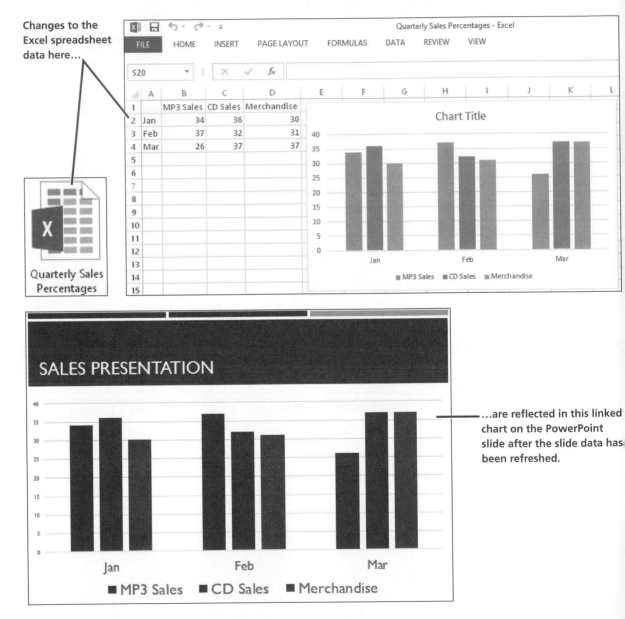

...are reflected in this linked chart on the PowerPoint slide after the slide data has been refreshed.

Changes to a linked Excel document *do not* result in automatic updating of the PowerPoint chart; you must manually refresh the PowerPoint chart's data to see the updated content.

Only Data Is Linked

A linked chart on a PowerPoint slide is linked to the Excel *data*, not to the Excel chart. The chart on the Excel spreadsheet simply establishes the initial link to its data. So, deleting or changing the format of the Excel chart has no effect on the PowerPoint chart. In the preceding illustration, notice that the formatting on the Excel chart is quite different from that on the PowerPoint slide. This independence allows PowerPoint to format the chart so it is consistent with the presentation theme's colors and fonts.

Linking Excel Charts

Your first step in linking to an Excel spreadsheet is to create the Excel spreadsheet that contains numerical data and an Excel chart. You simply copy and paste the chart (not the spreadsheet cells containing numerical data) from the Excel spreadsheet into your slide. The chart on the PowerPoint slide will be linked to the Excel spreadsheet's numerical data by default.

QUICK REFERENCE	LINKING CHARTS ON SLIDES
Task	**Procedure**
Link a chart	■ Select the Excel chart and choose Home→Clipboard→Copy.
	■ Select the desired PowerPoint slide and choose Home→Clipboard→Paste.
Edit linked data	■ Select the PowerPoint chart and choose Chart Tools→Design→Data→Edit Data.
	■ If available, the linked document will open. Edit the data in the Excel spreadsheet (not on the Excel chart), and save your changes.
Refresh chart data linked to an external file	■ Select the PowerPoint chart and choose Chart Tools→Design→Data→Refresh Data.
Repair a broken link	■ Select the chart, choose File→Info, and click the Edit Links to Files link.
	■ Click the Change Source button.
	■ Navigate to the source file, select it, and click Open.
	■ Click Close.

Paste Options

After you paste a chart from Excel, PowerPoint displays a set of three Paste Options buttons that allow you to control formatting of the pasted chart. The following table shows the function of each button.

PASTE OPTIONS		
Option	**Icon**	**What It Does**
Use Destination Theme & Embed Workbook		▪ Changes the formatting of the chart to match the slide theme. ▪ This is the default setting.
Keep Source Formatting & Embed Workbook		▪ Keeps the formatting of the Excel chart.
Picture		▪ Pastes the chart as a picture. The data is no longer editable.

DEVELOP YOUR SKILLS PP04-D04

Link to an Excel Chart

In this exercise, you will link to an existing Excel chart. You will then edit the Excel data to update the chart in PowerPoint.

1. Start **Microsoft Office Excel 2013**.

   The Excel program loads, and the Excel window appears.

2. Choose **Open Other Workbooks** from the bottom of the left column of Excel's Start screen.

3. Click **Computer→Browse**, navigate to the **PP2013 Lesson 04** folder, and open **PP04-D04-FinancialProjections**.

4. Click anywhere on the **Excel** chart to select it.

   A border appears around the chart to indicate that it has been selected.

5. Choose **Home→Clipboard→Copy**.

6. Close **Excel**.

   Excel closes, and you are returned to the PowerPoint window.

Link the Chart to PowerPoint

7. Save your PowerPoint presentation as **PP04-D04-Chart-[FirstInitialLastName]**.

8. Choose the **Year-To-Date Results** slide.

9. Choose **Home→Slides→New Slide** .

10. Choose **Home→Slides→ Layout →Title Only**.

    The new slide's layout is converted to the Title Only layout.

11. Click the title box of the new slide, type **Financial Projections**, and click below the title in a blank area of the slide.

The title box becomes deselected.

12. Choose **Home→Clipboard→Paste** 📋.

PowerPoint pastes the chart into the slide.

13. Tap Esc twice to dismiss the Paste Options buttons and accept the default setting.

Resize and Format the Chart

14. Follow these steps to resize the chart:

Ⓐ Point to the **bottom-left** sizing handle on the chart border until your mouse pointer becomes a white double-arrow, and then drag the border to the bottom-left corner of the slide.

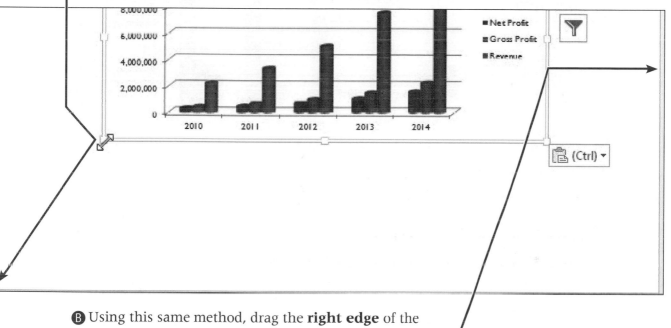

Ⓑ Using this same method, drag the **right edge** of the chart border until it snaps to the right edge of the slide.

The chart's text is too small to read comfortably. You will fix that in the next step.

15. Make sure the chart is selected and its border is displayed. Then choose **Home→ Font→Font Size menu ▼→20**.

All text on the chart is enlarged to size 20 and is easier to read. Your slide should resemble the following illustration.

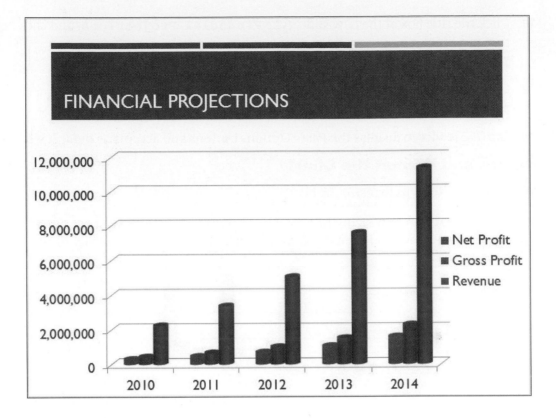

16. Save your presentation.

Effects of Linking

Video Library   http://labyrinthelab.com/videos   Video Number: PP13-V0405

When working with a linked chart, any changes made to the Excel spreadsheet are reflected in the PowerPoint chart, but not necessarily immediately. If the data is edited from within PowerPoint, the slide's chart is updated automatically. However, if the data is edited by opening Excel outside PowerPoint, the chart data must be refreshed in PowerPoint before the changes are visible on the slide. If you choose to paste unlinked, changes to the Excel spreadsheet will have no effect on the chart in the PowerPoint slide. If you attempt to edit linked chart data from within PowerPoint, a Linked Data window will open and present the linked spreadsheet, ready for editing. The Linked Data window will also give you the option to open the spreadsheet in Excel. If the linked spreadsheet cannot be found, you will not be able to edit the chart data until the link is repaired.

Edit Data in a Linked Spreadsheet

In this exercise, you will edit the data in a linked Excel spreadsheet.

1. Save your file as **PP04-D05-Chart-[FirstInitialLastName]**.

2. Select the **Financial Projections** slide. If necessary, click the chart to select it; choose **Chart Tools→Design→Data→Edit Data**.

   The Linked Data window opens the data source for the chart.

3. Follow these steps to edit the chart data:

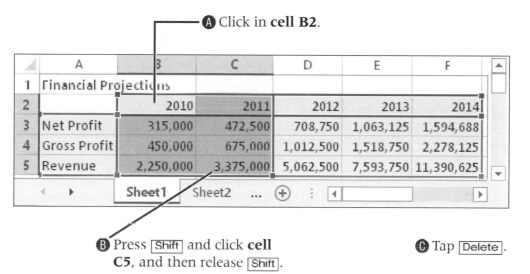

Ⓐ Click in **cell B2**.

Ⓑ Press ⌈Shift⌋ and click **cell C5**, and then release ⌈Shift⌋.

Ⓒ Tap ⌈Delete⌋.

   The selected data is deleted, and the change shows immediately on the slide, but there is a large gap on the chart where the data used to display. You will fix this in the next step.

4. Follow these steps to remove the empty cells:

Ⓐ Point to the **square handle** in the bottom-right corner of **cell A1** until your pointer is a **diagonal double-arrow**.

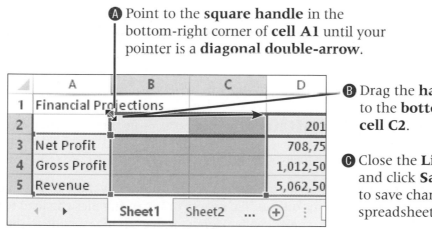

Ⓑ Drag the **handle** to the right, to the **bottom-right corner** of **cell C2**.

Ⓒ Close the **Linked Data** window and click **Save** when prompted to save changes to the Excel spreadsheet.

   The blank cells are removed from the chart on the slide.

5. Save the presentation.

Editing the Source (Linked) Document

Video Library   http://labyrinthelab.com/videos   Video Number: PP13-V0406

If you make a change to the source document outside PowerPoint, you must manually refresh the data to see the changes on the slide. Refreshing data is possible only if you have healthy links (PowerPoint can locate the source document).

DEVELOP YOUR SKILLS PP04-D06
Edit and Refresh the Data Source

In this exercise, you will edit and refresh the data source.

1. Start **Microsoft Office Excel 2013**.

2. Choose **Open Other Workbooks** from the bottom of the left column of Excel's Start screen.

3. Click **Computer→Browse**, navigate to the **PP2013 Lesson 04** folder, and open **PP04-D04-FinancialProjections**.

4. Click in **cell A5** and type `Big Money`.

   Excel replaces the word Revenue *with* Big Money.

5. Save the worksheet and exit **Excel**.

Refresh the Data Source

6. In **PowerPoint**, display the last slide, **Financial Projections**, if necessary.

   Notice that the chart legend to the right of the chart still shows the word Revenue. *It must be refreshed to reflect the changes in the data source.*

7. Save your presentation as **PP04-D06-Chart-[FirstInitialLastName]**.

8. Select the chart so the **Chart Tools** contextual tabs appear.

9. Choose **Chart Tools→Design→Data→Refresh Data** ⬜.

   PowerPoint refreshes the chart legend and now shows the phrase Big Money.

10. Save your presentation.

Maintaining Healthy Links

Video Library   http://labyrinthelab.com/videos   Video Number: PP13-V0407

Linked objects can reflect changes in the source document only if the link is maintained. Moving files to other locations on your file system or renaming files can lead to broken links, and your linked objects (like charts) will no longer reflect changes made to the source document.

If you try to edit chart data in PowerPoint and the Excel spreadsheet fails to open, you probably have a broken link.

Example

If you copied a chart from an Excel spreadsheet named Chart Data that was stored in a folder named My Excel Documents, PowerPoint would be looking for a file with that name in that location. If you moved the Excel file (or the containing folder) to another folder or changed its name, PowerPoint would no longer be able to find it; therefore, any changes made to the spreadsheet would have no effect on the chart in PowerPoint. And if you tried to edit the data from within PowerPoint, PowerPoint would not be able to find the Excel spreadsheet and thus would not be able to edit the data.

The following figure illustrates the prompt that PowerPoint displays if you break a link to an external file—for example, if you move or rename the data source file, and then try to edit a chart from PowerPoint.

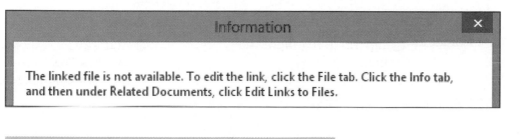

DEVELOP YOUR SKILLS PP04-D07
Break and Repair a Link

In this exercise, you will break a link by renaming the linked data file, and then you will repair the link from within PowerPoint.

1. Save your file as **PP04-D07-Chart-[FirstInitialLastName]**.

2. **Minimize** ⬜ the PowerPoint window to the taskbar.

3. Follow the instructions for your version of Windows to open a window for your file storage location.

   ■ **Windows 7:** Use **Start→Computer** and open your file storage location.

   ■ **Windows 8:** Use the **File Explorer icon** on the **taskbar** to open a folder window and then open your file storage location.

4. Open the **PP2013 Lesson 04** folder.

In the next step, you will rename a file. Most windows systems hide the ends of filenames (called extensions). If they are visible, take care not to change them.

5. Follow these steps to rename the Excel worksheet file:

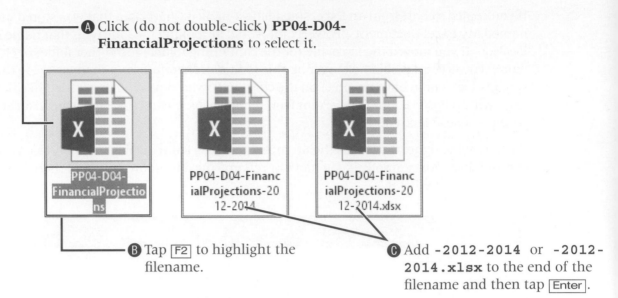

Ⓐ Click (do not double-click) **PP04-D04-FinancialProjections** to select it.

Ⓑ Tap [F2] to highlight the filename.

Ⓒ Add **-2012-2014** or **-2012-2014.xlsx** to the end of the filename and then tap [Enter].

If the filename displayed the .xlsx file extension, be sure your new filename looks like PP04-D04-FinancialProjections-2012-2014.xlsx. Otherwise, your filename should simply be PP04-D04-FinancialProjections-2012-2014. By renaming the source document, you have broken its link to PowerPoint.

6. Close the folder window and then click the **PowerPoint** button on the Windows taskbar to restore PowerPoint to the screen.

7. Click the chart to select it, if necessary.

8. Choose **Chart Tools→Design→Data→Edit Data**.

You receive an error. PowerPoint is looking for a source document named PP04-D04-FinancialProjections, but you changed the name of the file.

9. Click **OK** in the error box.

Fix the Broken Link

10. Choose **File→Info** and then click **Edit Links to Files** at the bottom-right of the right column.

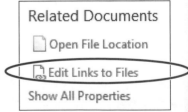

The Links dialog box appears, listing all links to external files from the presentation. In this case, there is just one linked item, the Excel spreadsheet.

11. Click **Change Source**.

12. In the **Change Source** dialog box, navigate to the **PP2013 Lesson 04** folder, select **PP04-D04-FinancialProjections-2012-2014**, and click **Open**.

PowerPoint updates the link. There may not be enough space in the dialog box to make the new name visible.

13. Click ⟨ Close ⟩ to close the **Links** dialog box.

You have reestablished the link between the PowerPoint chart and the Excel source document.

Test the Repaired Link

14. Click **Back** ⬅ to close Backstage view; click the chart to select it, if necessary.

The chart must be selected in order to display the Chart Tools contextual tabs.

15. Choose **Chart Tools→Design→Data→Edit Data** 📝.

The source document opens, ready to edit.

16. Click in **cell A5**. Then type **Revenue** and tap Enter.

Excel replaces Big Money *with the new word, and the change is immediately visible on the slide.*

17. Close the **Linked Data** window and click **Save** when prompted.

18. Save your presentation.

Creating SmartArt Diagrams

Video Library   http://labyrinthelab.com/videos   Video Number: PP13-V0408

SmartArt graphics are diagrams that automatically resize to accommodate the text within and allow the average user to enhance slides with visually appealing figures without having to learn advanced graphics software. With SmartArt, you simply select the type of diagram you'd like to create and type your text. The SmartArt diagram automatically sizes and flows your text. It also inherits colors and 3-D effects from your document theme. The resulting diagrams can help crystallize concepts in your presentation so that the audience will clearly understand your ideas. Using SmartArt, you can add graphics to your presentations, such as the following:

- Organization charts
- Flowcharts
- Colorful lists
- And many other sophisticated graphics

Inserting and Formatting SmartArt Graphics

Most slide layouts include an Insert SmartArt Graphic icon. Alternatively, SmartArt can be inserted at any time via the Ribbon. When you click the Insert SmartArt Graphic icon, the Choose a SmartArt Graphic dialog box appears. You can choose a diagram type from the gallery and then construct the diagram directly on the slide. PowerPoint displays examples and descriptions of the various SmartArt graphics as you select them in the gallery.

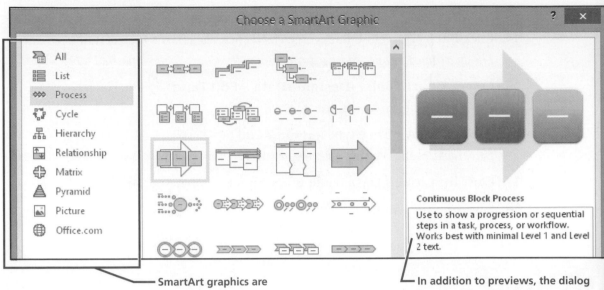

SmartArt graphics are categorized by chart type.

In addition to previews, the dialog box describes the best uses of each type of diagram.

SMARTART GRAPHIC CHART TYPES

Graphic Category	Usage
List	Show nonsequential or grouped blocks of information
Process	Show a progression or sequential flow of data
Cycle	Show a continuing sequence of stages
Hierarchy	Show hierarchal relationships
Relationship	Show ideas, show interlocking or overlapping information, or show relationships to a central idea
Matrix	Show the relationships of components to a whole
Pyramid	Show proportional, interconnected, hierarchical, or containment relationships
Picture	Show a variety of information by using a central picture or several accent pictures
Office.com	Includes graphics from a variety of categories that can be downloaded from the Office.com website

Example

As you create your presentation, you need to include an organization chart that features the key players in your project or the leadership team of your organization. You give the command to insert a SmartArt graphic, browse through the Hierarchy list, and then choose an organization chart. You type the various organizational units in the SmartArt's text box. Three minutes later, you're finished!

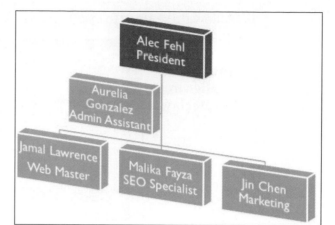

SmartArt organization charts automatically create and align boxes and lines as you type the names of the persons and departments.

QUICK REFERENCE	INSERTING SMARTART
Task	**Procedure**
Insert a new SmartArt graphic	■ Click the Insert SmartArt Graphic ⊞ icon in the center of a slide, or choose Insert→Illustrations→SmartArt.
	■ In the Choose a SmartArt Graphic dialog box, select a category of graphics to view the thumbnails and samples.
	■ Select a thumbnail and click OK.
Edit and format SmartArt	■ Select the SmartArt graphic (or any shape that is part of the graphic).
	■ Drag the handles on the shape's border to resize the shape.
	■ Make changes to the graphic's color, effects, or layout by choosing the commands from SmartArt Tools→Design or SmartArt Tools→Format.
	■ Reset a SmartArt graphic to its default settings by choosing SmartArt Tools→Design→Reset→Reset Graphic.
Add a new element to a SmartArt graphic	■ Select one of the shapes in the SmartArt graphic.
	■ Choose SmartArt Tools→Design→Create Graphic→Add Shape menu ▼ and select where you want the new shape to appear relative to the selected shape.

Set Up an Organization Chart

In this exercise, you will create an organization chart in PowerPoint, adding text to the various levels of the chart.

1. Save your file as **PP04-D08-Chart-[FirstInitialLastName]**.

2. Select the **Financial Projections** slide and choose **Home→Slides→New Slide**.

3. Choose **Home→Slides→** ⊞ Layout ▾ **→Title and Content**.

4. Type **Our Management Team** in the Title placeholder.

5. Click the **Insert SmartArt Graphic** ⊞ icon in the middle of the slide.
   The Choose a SmartArt Graphic dialog box appears.

6. Follow these steps to insert an organization chart:

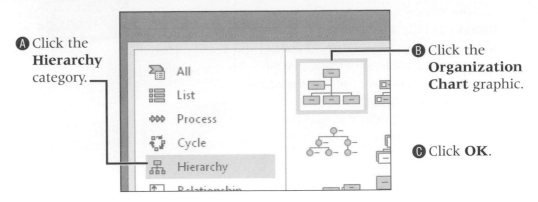

Ⓐ Click the **Hierarchy** category.

Ⓑ Click the **Organization Chart** graphic.

Ⓒ Click **OK**.

A sample organization chart is inserted. The contextual SmartArt Tools tabs appear on the right side of the Ribbon, including Design and Format.

Add Text

7. Follow these steps to add text to the organization chart:

Ⓐ If the Text pane appears with the SmartArt graphic, click its **Close** button. It is easier to type directly in the chart.

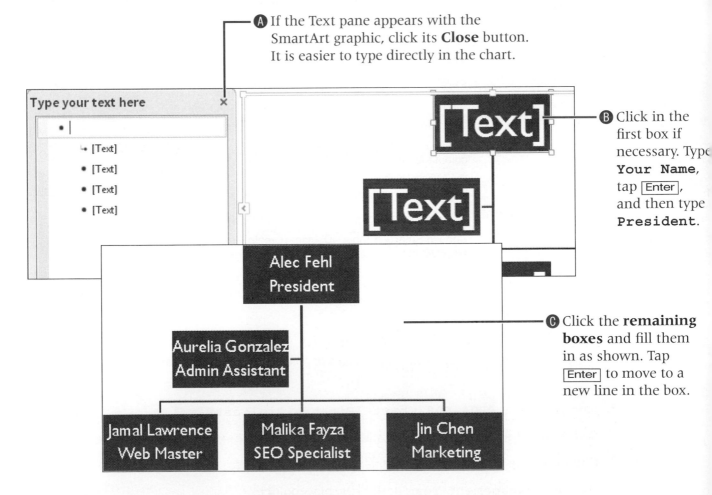

Ⓑ Click in the first box if necessary. Type **Your Name**, tap Enter, and then type **President**.

Ⓒ Click the **remaining boxes** and fill them in as shown. Tap Enter to move to a new line in the box.

8. Save your presentation.

Formatting SmartArt

Video Library   http://labyrinthelab.com/videos   Video Number: PP-13-V0409

After a SmartArt graphic has been added to a slide, you can format its colors and other effects. For example, you can customize the graphic's text formatting, color scheme, and other features. Many SmartArt graphics have 3-D schemes and other cool effects that you can experiment with to add visual impact to a slide.

Adding Elements to SmartArt

You can also add elements to an original SmartArt graphic. For example, an organization chart might need a new branch for adding a department or lateral relationship. You may insert additional shapes above, below, or next to an existing shape. The SmartArt graphic will automatically resize itself and scale its text to accommodate the extra shapes.

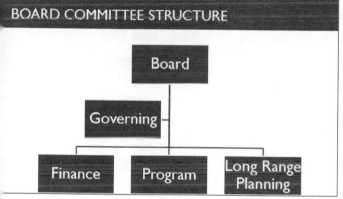

When a shape was inserted next to the Long Range Planning box, PowerPoint automatically resized the SmartArt to make room for the new, blank shape.

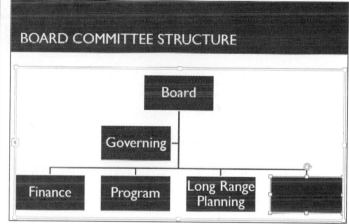

Add Shapes and Format SmartArt

In this exercise, you will add a new position in the organization chart and enhance its appearance with a different formatting effect.

1. Save your file as **PP04-D09-Chart-[FirstInitialLastName]**.

2. Click in the **Malika Fayza** box in the organization chart.

   This selects the appropriate box so you can add another shape beside it.

3. Choose **SmartArt Tools→Design→Create Graphic→Add Shape menu ▾→Add Shape After**.

   A new box is added to the right of the Malika Fayza box and is ready to accept text.

4. Type **Brett Schneider** in the new box, tap Enter to move to a second line in the box, and type **Fulfillment**.

PowerPoint 2013

Format the Chart

5. Follow these steps to format the chart:

Ⓐ Choose **SmartArt Tools→Design→ SmartArt Styles→More.**

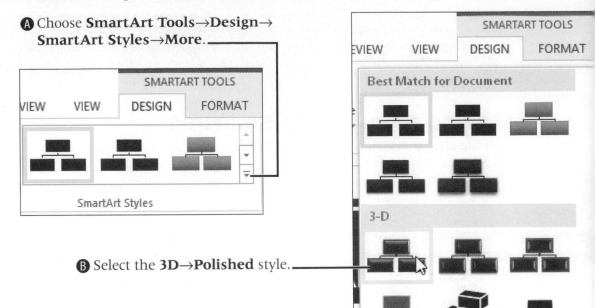

Ⓑ Select the **3D→Polished** style.

The Polished style is applied to every box in the chart.

6. Follow these steps to change the chart's colors:

Ⓐ Choose **SmartArt Tools→Design→ SmartArt Styles→Change Colors.**

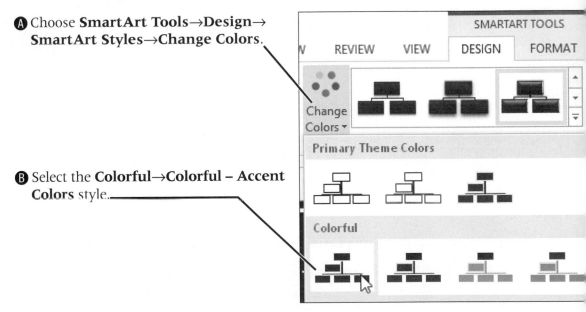

Ⓑ Select the **Colorful→Colorful – Accent Colors** style.

The organization chart should resemble the following illustration.

7. Save the presentation and then exit **PowerPoint**.

Concepts Review

To check your knowledge of the key concepts introduced in this lesson, complete the Concepts Review quiz by choosing the appropriate access option below.

If you are...	Then access the quiz by...
Using the Labyrinth Video Library	Going to http://labyrinthelab.com/videos
Using eLab	Logging in, choosing Content, and navigating to the Concepts Review quiz for this lesson
Not using the Labyrinth Video Library or eLab	Going to the student resource center for this book

Reinforce Your Skills

Work with an Embedded Chart

In this exercise, you will create a new presentation for Kids for Change and add a chart slide to the presentation. You will change the chart type to a pie chart to better display the data.

Begin a New Presentation and Insert a Chart

1. Start **PowerPoint** and click the **Blank Presentation** icon.

2. Save your file as `PP04-R01-Members-[FirstInitialLastName]` in the **PP2013 Lesson 04** folder.

3. Choose **Design→Themes** and select the **Slice** theme.

   Remember, the default themes are listed in alphabetical order. Point to a theme thumbnail and pause for a moment to view the theme name in a pop-up ToolTip.

4. In the **Title** box, type `Kids for Change`.

5. Click in the **Subtitle** box and type `New Members`.

6. Choose **Home→Slides→New Slide** and type `2013 New Members` in the title box.

7. Click the **Insert Chart** icon in the content placeholder box.

Modify a Chart

8. Choose the **3-D Clustered Bar** chart type and click **OK**.

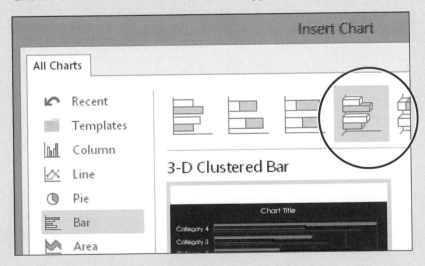

You will now enter the chart data.

9. Enter the data in **columns A and B** as shown and then delete the data in **columns C and D**. (The column headings will default to Column 1 and Column 2.)

	A	B	C	D
1		2013	Column1	Column2
2	9 and under	21		
3	10 to 12	36		
4	13 to 15	36		
5	16 to 17	47		
6				

10. Drag the bottom-right handle of cell D5 to the bottom-right corner of **cell B5** to remove the empty columns from the chart.

	A	B	C	D
1		2013	Column1	Column2
2	9 and under	21		
3	10 to 12	36		
4	13 to 15	36		
5	16 to 17	47		
6				

11. Close the **Chart** window.

    In the next steps, you will edit the chart data.

12. Click the chart on the slide to select it, if necessary, and choose **Chart Tools→Design→ Data →Edit Data**.

13. Click in **cell B4**, type **34**, and tap [Enter] to change the value.

14. Click the chart to display its border, and then click the chart border.

15. Close the **Chart** window.

    The chart bars are updated, and the 13 to 15 bar is now shorter than the 10 to 12 bar.

    Because the chart shows pieces of a whole (total new members broken down by age), a pie chart is a better choice, so you will change the chart type.

16. Choose **Chart Tools→Design→Type→Change Chart Type**.

17. Choose **3-D Pie** as the chart type and click **OK**.

Change Chart Layout and Size

18. Choose **Chart Tools→Design→Chart Layouts→Quick Layout→Layout 1**.

The chart layout is changed, and percentages now display on each pie slice.

Change Chart Style

19. Choose **Chart Tools→Design→Chart Styles→Style 2**.

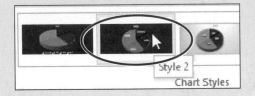

Change Chart Size

20. Drag the **bottom-right handle** of the chart's border to the **bottom-right corner** of the slide.

21. Drag the **left-center handle** of the chart's border to the right until the chart no longer overlaps the slide title.

22. Click the chart's title, **2013**, and tap `Delete`.

23. Choose **Home→Font→Font Size menu ▼→20**.

24. Save the changes and then exit **PowerPoint**. Submit your final file based on the guidelines provided by your instructor.

    To view examples of how your file or files should look at the end of this exercise, go to the student resource center.

REINFORCE YOUR SKILLS PP04-R02

Work with a Linked Chart and SmartArt

In this exercise, you will link to an external data source, repair a broken link to a linked chart, and add SmartArt to display member and participant numbers.

Link to and Format an Excel Chart

1. Start **PowerPoint**. Open **PP04-R02-Projections** from the **PP2013 Lesson 04** folder and save it as `PP04-R02-Projections-[FirstInitialLastName]`.

2. Display slide 2 and choose **Home→Slides→New Slide**.

3. Type **Participant Projections** as the slide title.

4. Start **Excel**. Open **PP04-R02-Projections** from the **PP2013 Lesson 04** folder.

5. Click the chart on the Excel spreadsheet to select it.

6. Choose **Home→Clipboard→Copy**.

7. Exit **Excel**.

8. Click the **PowerPoint slide** so that the slide title is deselected.

9. Choose **Home→Clipboard→Paste**.

10. Drag the **top-left handle** of the chart's border to the **top-left corner** of the slide.

11. Drag the **center-right handle** of the chart's border toward the right until the chart is as wide as possible but the chart buttons are still visible.

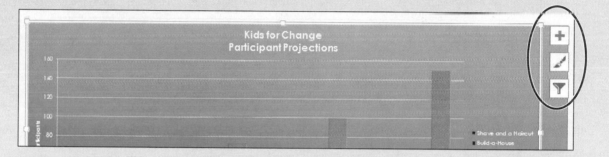

12. Click the **Chart Elements** button to the right of the chart.

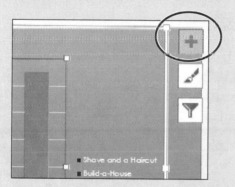

13. Choose to not display the **Chart Title** and remove the checkmark from **Primary Horizontal**.

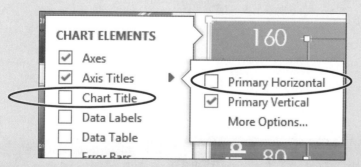

14. Tap Esc to close the **Chart Elements** menu.

15. Click the chart to display its border, and then click the chart border.

16. Choose **Home→Font→Font Size menu ▼→28**.

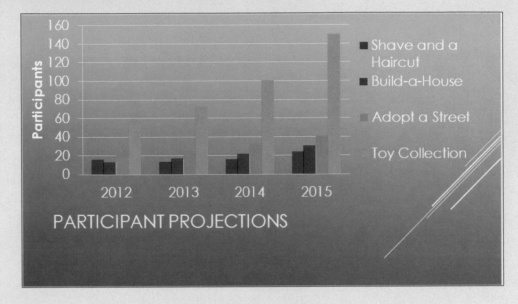

Edit a Linked Data Source and Repair a Broken Link

17. Display slide 2, **2013 New Members**.

18. Click the chart to select it.

19. Choose **Chart Tools→Design→Data→Edit Data**.
    A message appears, informing you that PowerPoint cannot find the linked Excel spreadsheet.

20. Click **OK** to close the Information box.

21. Choose **File→Info** and then click the **Edit Links to Files** link at the bottom of the right column.
    You will now perform the steps necessary to repair the link.

22. Click the entry that ends with **2013members.xlsx** and then click **Change Source**.

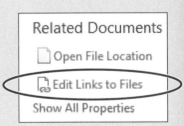

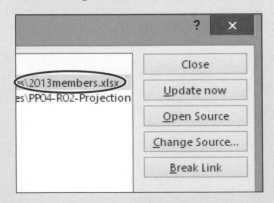

23. Browse to the **PP2013 Lesson 04** folder, if necessary. Select the **PP04-R02-Members** file and click **Open**.

24. Click **Close** to close the **Links** dialog box.

25. Click **Back** 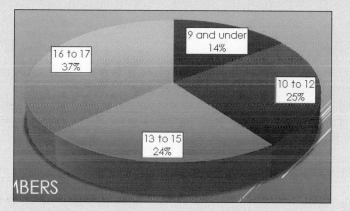 to exit Backstage view.

    Now that the link is fixed, you will edit the data.

26. Choose **Chart Tools→Design→Data→Edit Data**.

27. Click **cell B5**, type **53**, and tap Enter.

    The chart on the slide is immediately updated.

28. Close the **Linked Data** window and click **Save** when prompted.

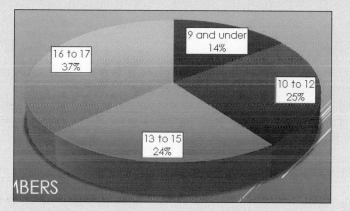

Insert SmartArt

29. Display slide 3, **Participant Projections**.

30. Choose **Home→Slides→New Slide**.

31. Choose **Home→Slides→Layout→Title and Content**.

32. Type **Current Members** as the slide title.

33. Click the **SmartArt** icon on the slide.

34. Click the **Process** category, choose **Step Up Process**, and then click **OK**.

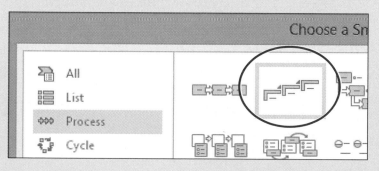

Although the Process category is typically used to show sequential steps, you will use this graphic to show age groups of members, from least members to the most members.

35. If the text box appears next to the SmartArt graphic, close it.

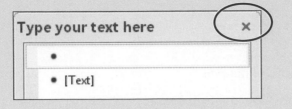

36. Type the text in each section of the SmartArt graphic as shown:

Format and Add Elements to SmartArt

37. With the SmartArt graphic selected, choose **SmartArt Tools→Design→SmartArt Styles→More→Best Match for Document→Intense Effect**.

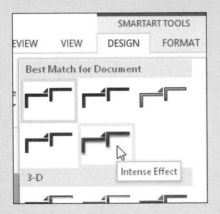

38. Click the text **Teens** to select that SmartArt text box.

39. Chose **SmartArt Tools→Design→Create Graphic→Add Shape menu ▼→Add Shape Before**.

40. Type **Under 10** in the new text box.

41. Save the changes and then exit **PowerPoint**. Submit your final file based on the guidelines provided by your instructor.

To view examples of how your file or files should look at the end of this exercise, go to the student resource center.

Work with Charts and SmartArt

In this exercise, you will use charts and SmartArt to compare Kids for Change events from several communities.

Begin a New Presentation and Create an Embedded Chart

1. Start **PowerPoint** and click the **Blank Presentation** icon.

2. Save your file as `PP04-R03-Events-[FirstInitialLastName]` in your **PP2013 Lesson 04** folder.

3. Choose **Design→Themes** and select the **Integral** theme.

4. In the **Title** box, type `Kids for Change`.

5. Click in the **Subtitle** box and type `2013 Events`.

6. Choose **Home→Slides→New Slide**.

7. Type `Event Totals` as the title.

8. Click the **Insert Chart** ▮▮ icon on the slide.

Modify a Chart Type

9. Click the **Bar** category, click the **Clustered Bar** chart type, and click **OK**.

10. Type the following data in rows 1 and 2 of the Chart spreadsheet:

◢	A	B	C	D	E	F
1		Westville	North Haven	Sunny Downs	Goodview	Echo Falls
2	2013	8	12	2	6	8

11. Drag the **bottom-right handle of cell F5** up to the **bottom-right corner of cell F2** to exclude rows 3 through 5.

12. Close the **Chart** window.

    You will now work to format the chart.

13. Choose **Chart Tools→Design→Chart Styles→More→Style 4**.

14. Choose **Chart Tools→Design→Quick Layout→Layout 2**.

15. Click the **Chart Elements** button to the right of the chart.

16. Uncheck **Axes** and then tap [Esc] to close the **Chart Elements** menu.

17. Click the **chart title** and type `2013 Events`.

18. Drag the right edge of the chart until it snaps to the right edge of the slide to widen it.

19. Choose **Home→Font→Font Size menu ▼→28**.

Edit Chart Data and Change a Chart Type

20. Choose **Chart Tools→Design→Data→Edit Data** 📊.

21. Click **cell C2**, type **14**, and tap Enter.

22. Close the **Chart** window.

23. Choose **Chart Tools→Design→Type→Change Chart Type**.

24. Choose the last chart type in the **Bar** category, **3-D 100% Stacked Bar**, and click **OK**.

25. Drag the **bottom-left handle** of the chart's border to the **bottom-left corner** of the slide.

26. Drag the **top-middle handle** of the chart's border up until the **top edge** of the chart touches the bottom of the slide's title text.

Change Chart Colors

27. Choose **Chart Tools→Design→Chart Styles→Change Colors→Color 2**.

Link to an Excel Chart

28. Start **Excel** and choose **Open Other Workbooks**.

29. Browse to your **PP2013 Lesson 04** folder and double-click the **PP04-R03-Events** workbook file.

30. Click the **chart** to select it and then choose **Home→Clipboard→Copy**.

31. Exit **Excel**.

32. In PowerPoint, choose **Home→Slides→New Slide**.

33. Type **Event Popularity** as the slide title.

34. Choose **Home→Slides→Layout→Title Only**.

35. Choose **Home→Clipboard→Paste**.

36. Drag the **bottom-left handle** of the chart's border to the **bottom-left corner** of the slide.

37. Drag the **top-right handle** of the chart's border up and to the right, until the top edge of the chart touches the bottom of the title text and the chart is as wide as possible while keeping the chart buttons visible, as in the following figure.

38. Click the **chart title** and tap Delete.

39. Choose **Home→Font→Font Size menu ▼→24**.

Break a Link

40. Minimize **PowerPoint**.

41. Use **Computer** or **File Explorer** to navigate to the **PP2013 Lesson 04** folder and locate the **PP04-R03-Events** workbook.

42. Click the **PP04-R03-Events** workbook to select it and tap F2 to highlight the filename.

43. Type **PP04-R03-Events2013** and tap Enter to rename the file.

Fix a Broken Link and Edit a Linked Data Source

44. Click the **PowerPoint** button on the **Windows taskbar** to restore PowerPoint.

45. Click the chart to select it, if necessary.

46. Choose **Chart Tools→Design→Data→Edit Data**.

47. Click **OK** to dismiss the **Information** dialog box.

48. Choose **File→Info→Edit Links to Files**.

49. Click **Change Source**, navigate to the **PP2013 Lesson 04** folder, and double-click the **PP04-R03-Events2013** workbook.

50. Click the **Close** button.

51. Click the **Back** button at the top of the left column to exit Backstage view.

At the time of this writing, a bug in PowerPoint causes the chart to no longer display even though the data is still linked. It may be necessary to delete and copy/paste the chart again if Microsoft hasn't released an update yet.

52. Choose **Chart Tools→Design→Data→Edit Data**.

53. Click **cell E2** and type 0.

54. Click **cell E3** and type 1.

55. Click **cell E5** and type 1.

56. Close the **Linked Data** window and click **Save** when prompted.

Edit and Refresh External Data

57. Start **Excel** and choose **Open Other Workbooks**.

58. Browse to your **PP2013 Lesson 04** folder and double-click **PP04-R03-Events2013**.

59. Click **cell C9** and type **0**, and then click **cell C8** and type **4**.

60. Click **cell E9** and type **0**, and then click **cell E8** and type **3**.

61. Save the **Excel** workbook and exit **Excel**.

62. In **PowerPoint**, choose **Chart Tools→Design→Data→Refresh Data**.

Insert SmartArt

63. Choose **Home→Slides→New Slide**.

64. Choose **Home→Slides→Layout→Title and Content**.

65. Type **Most Popular** as the **slide title**.

66. Click the **Insert SmartArt** icon on the slide.

67. Choose the **Pyramid** category, the **Basic Pyramid** graphic, and then click **OK**.

68. Click the **bottom text box** of the pyramid and type **Bully No More**.

69. Click the **middle text box** of the pyramid and type **Adopt a Street**.

70. Click the **top text box** of the pyramid and type **Toy Collection**.

Format SmartArt

71. Choose **SmartArt Tools→Design→SmartArt Styles→More→3-D→Brick Scene**.

72. Choose **SmartArt Tools→Design→SmartArt Styles→Change Colors→Colorful→Colorful – Accent Colors**.

73. Drag the **top-center handle** of the SmartArt border to the **top** of the slide.

74. Drag the **bottom-right handle** of the SmartArt border to the **bottom-right corner** of the slide.

Add Elements to SmartArt

75. Click in the **bottom text box** of the pyramid.

76. Choose **SmartArt Tools→Design→Create Graphic→Add Shape menu ▼→Add Shape After**.

77. Type **Diversity Festival** in the bottom text box.

78. Save the changes and then exit **PowerPoint**. Submit your final file based on the guidelines provided by your instructor.

Apply Your Skills

Insert and Format an Embedded Chart

In this exercise, you will create a new presentation for Universal Corporate Events and add a nicely formatted, embedded chart to the presentation.

Begin a New Presentation and Create an Embedded Chart

1. Start **PowerPoint** and create a new, blank presentation.

2. Save the file as **PP04-A01-Review-[FirstInitialLastName]** in your **PP2013 Lesson 04** folder.

3. Apply the **Retrospect** theme.

4. Type the title **Universal Corporate Events** and the subtitle **Quarterly Review**.

5. Add a new slide with the title **Quarterly Breakdown**.

6. Insert a **Clustered Column** chart.

7. Enter this data:

	A	B	C	D	E
1		Jan-Mar	Apr-Jun	Jul-Sep	Oct-Dec
2	Total Events	22	72	34	115

8. Drag the data's border so that only **rows 1 and 2** are included and then close the **Chart window**.

Edit Chart Data and Change Chart Type, Layout, and Style

9. Edit the chart's data so that **cell B2** has a value of **18** and **cell E2** has a value of **132**.

10. Change the chart type to **3-D Clustered Column**.

11. Change the chart layout to **Layout 2**.

12. Change the chart style to **Style 11**.

Select Chart Elements and Change Chart Size and Text

13. Remove the chart's **Title, Gridlines, and Primary Vertical Axis label**.

14. Resize the chart so it fills the maximum area of the slide without overlapping the slide title.

15. Set the font size of the chart to **24**.

16. Click the number **18** above the first bar, locate the **Chart Tools→Format→Shape Styles gallery**, and choose the first style, **Colored Outline – Black, Dark 1**.

17. Apply the same **Shape Style** to the numbers on top of the remaining bars.

18. Save the changes and then exit **PowerPoint**. Submit your final file based on the guidelines provided by your instructor.

    To view examples of how your file or files should look at the end of this exercise, go to the student resource center.

Work with Linked Charts and SmartArt

In this exercise, you will add a chart linked to an external data source. You will also add and format SmartArt.

Link and Format a Chart

1. Start **PowerPoint**. Open **PP04-A02-Projections** from the **PP2013 Lesson 04** folder and save it as **PP04-A02-Projections-[FirstInitialLastName]**.

2. Add a new third slide with the title **Event Projections**.

3. Start **Excel**. Open **PP04-A02-Projections** from the **PP2013 Lesson 04** folder.

4. Copy the chart from the **Excel spreadsheet** and paste it onto the **Event Projections PowerPoint slide**. Then exit **Excel**.

5. Resize the chart so it fills the maximum area of the slide without overlapping the slide title.

6. Use the **Chart Elements** button to display **Data Labels**.

7. Set the font size of the chart to **28**.

8. Change the colors of the chart to **Color 2**.

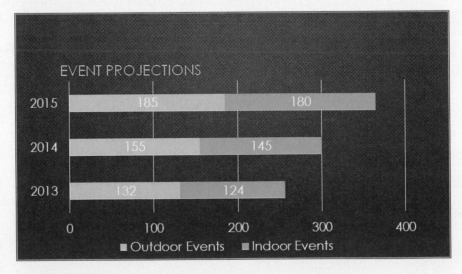

Fix a Broken Link and Edit a Linked Data Source

9. Select the chart on **slide 2** and attempt to edit the data.

   You must repair the broken link before you can edit the data.

10. Edit the link to the chart so that instead of pointing to the **Events2013.xlsx** workbook, the chart points to **PP04-A02-Events**.

11. Edit the chart data so that **cell B2** (Award Ceremonies value) is **67** instead of 7.

Insert and Modify SmartArt

12. Add a new fourth slide with the **Title and Content** layout.

13. Use `Growth` as the slide title.

14. Add the **Process→Upward Arrow** SmartArt graphic to the slide.

15. Type `Improved Catering` in the **left text box**, `Economic Transportation` in the **middle text box**, and `Building Ownership` in the **right text box**.

16. Add a shape **after** the right-most text box with the text `Growth in 2014`.

17. Use the **SmartArt Tools→Design** tab to apply the **Colorful→Colorful Range – Accent Colors 3-4** colors to the SmartArt.

18. Use the **SmartArt Tools→Design** tab to apply the **3-D→Polished** SmartArt Style.

19. Select each text box in the SmartArt graphic and use the Font Color menu on the **Home** tab to change all the SmartArt text colors to **Green, Accent 3**.

20. Enlarge the graphic and make the text **bold**.

21. Save the changes and then exit **PowerPoint**. Submit your final file based on the guidelines provided by your instructor.

    To view examples of how your file or files should look at the end of this exercise, go to the student resource center.

APPLY YOUR SKILLS PP04-A03

Work with Charts and SmartArt

In this exercise, you will add and format charts and SmartArt to the Universal Corporate Events presentation.

Begin a New Presentation and Create an Embedded Chart

1. Start **PowerPoint**. Create a new, blank presentation and save it to your **PP2013 Lesson 04** folder as `PP04-A03-Supplies-[FirstInitialLastName]`.

2. Apply the **Ion** theme with the **fourth (orange) variant**.

3. Give the slide a title of `Universal Corporate Events` and a subtitle of `Supplies`.

4. Change the font size of the slide title to **40**.

5. Add a second slide with the title `Projected Catering Supplies for 2014` and use the icon on the slide to insert a **Clustered Column** chart.

6. Type the following data in the spreadsheet and remove **row 5** from the chart data.

◢	A	B	C	D
1		2012	2013	2014
2	Bamboo Skewers	1250	1300	1500
3	Foil Pans	251	372	475
4	Foil Trays	175	310	400
5	Category 4	4.5	2.8	5

Format a Chart and Edit Chart Data

7. Resize the chart so it fills the maximum area of the slide without overlapping the slide title.

8. Delete the **chart title**.

9. Apply **Chart Style 6**.

10. Use the **Chart Elements** button to display the **Data Labels** and hide the **Gridlines** and **Primary Vertical axis**.

11. Apply the **Color 3** colors to the chart and increase the **font size** to **24**.

12. Edit the chart data to include the following data in **row 5**. Be sure to extend the data's border so row 5 is included in the chart.

3	Foil Pans	251	372	475
4	Foil Trays	175	310	400
5	Sterno Cans	200	250	290

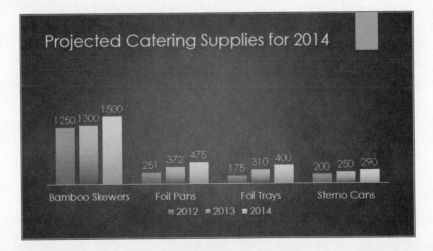

Link a Chart and Change and Format a Linked Chart

13. Create a new third slide with the title `Popular Dishes` and set the slide layout to **Title Only**.

14. Start **Excel**. Open **PP04-A03-Favorites** from the **PP2013 Lesson 04** folder.

15. Copy the chart from the **Excel spreadsheet** and paste it onto the **Popular Dishes PowerPoint slide**. Exit **Excel**.

16. Resize the chart so it fills the maximum area of the slide without overlapping the slide title.

17. Change the chart type to **3-D Pie**.

18. Apply a **Chart Style** of **Style 1** to the chart.

19. Change the layout of the chart to **Layout 1**.

20. Use the **Chart Elements button** next to the chart to hide the **Chart Title** and show **Data Labels→Data Callout**.

21. Set the font size of the chart to **24**.

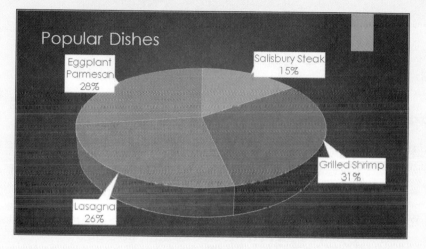

Break and Fix a Link and Edit a Linked Data Source

22. Minimize **PowerPoint** and use **Computer** or **File Explorer** to navigate to the **PP2013 Lesson 04** folder and locate the **PP04-A03-Favorites** workbook.

23. Rename the file `PP04-A03-Favorites2013`.

24. Restore **PowerPoint**, click the chart, and attempt to edit the data.

25. Dismiss the **Information** dialog box.

26. Edit the link to the spreadsheet so PowerPoint can find the newly named **PP04-A03-Favorites2013** file.

    At the time of this writing, a bug in PowerPoint causes the chart to no longer display even though the data is still linked. It may be necessary to delete and copy/paste the chart again if Microsoft hasn't released an update yet.

27. Edit the chart data to show **1938** servings of **Grilled Shrimp**.

28. Save the presentation and exit **PowerPoint**.

Edit and Refresh External Data

29. Start **Excel** and open **PP04-A03-Favorites2013**.

30. Change the **Lasagna** servings to **1164** and the **Eggplant** servings to **1223**.

31. Save the **Excel** workbook and exit **Excel**.

32. Start **PowerPoint** and open **PP04-A03-Supplies-[FirstInitialLastName]**.

33. Refresh the data on **slide 3**.

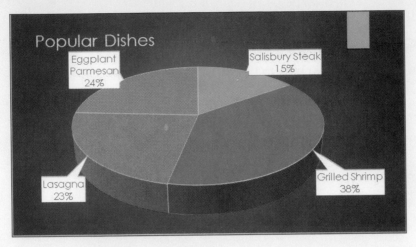

Insert and Format SmartArt

34. Create a **new fourth slide** with the **Title and Content** layout and a **slide title** of `Catering Goals`.

35. Insert a **Relationship→Radial Cycle** graphic.

36. In the **top circle**, type `Flavorful`. In the **right circle**, type `Healthy`. In the **left circle**, type `Economical`. In the **inner circle**, type `Respected and Desired`.

37. Click in the **bottom circle**, click the **text box's border**, and tap Delete.

38. Apply the **3-D→Polished** SmartArt Style to the graphic.

39. Apply the **Primary Theme Colors→Dark 2 Fill** color.

40. Resize the SmartArt so it fills the maximum area of the slide without overlapping the slide title.

41. **Bold** the text and add a **text shadow**.

42. Save the changes and then exit **PowerPoint**. Submit your final file based on the guidelines provided by your instructor.

Extend Your Skills

In the course of working through the Extend Your Skills exercises, you will think critically as you use the skills taught in the lesson to complete the assigned projects. To evaluate your mastery and completion of the exercises, your instructor may use a rubric, with which more points are allotted according to performance characteristics. (The more you do, the more you earn!) Ask your instructor how your work will be evaluated.

PP04-E01 That's the Way I See It

Charts are often used in advertising to exaggerate results. Interview ten people and ask them to choose their favorite item from a list of three things (such as ice-cream flavors, cell-phone brands, or musical genres). Create a new presentation with an appropriate title and subtitle on the first slide. Apply an appropriate design theme. On a second slide, add a title and insert a pie chart that displays your survey results. Label each pie slice with a percentage to exaggerate the results. (Showing 60 percent prefer chocolate is more impressive than showing only six people!) Use the Chart Elements button to experiment with showing/hiding chart elements. Ensure that all information displays without looking too busy, and that the chart and labels are large enough for an audience to see when the slide show is presented. Add a third slide that displays the survey results as a visually appealing SmartArt graphic. Save the file as **PP04-E01-Survey-[FirstInitialLastName]** in the **PP2013 Lesson 04** folder.

You will be evaluated based on the inclusion of all elements specified, your ability to follow directions, your ability to apply newly learned skills to a real-world situation, your creativity, and the relevance of your topic and/or data choice(s). Submit your final file based on the guidelines provided by your instructor.

PP04-E02 Be Your Own Boss

In this exercise, you will create a presentation to show the flowers planted by your company, Blue Jean Landscaping, as well as a graphic to explain the basics of garden health for your clients. Create a new, blank presentation named **PP04-E02-BlueJeanChart-[FirstInitialLastName]** in the **PP2013 Lesson 04** folder. Apply the Wisp theme, the title **Blue Jean Landscaping**, and the subtitle **Flowers Planted**. Create a second slide with the Title Only layout and the title **Flowers Planted**. In Excel, create a new, blank spreadsheet that lists flowers down column A and numbers down column B. The spreadsheet should show **Roses – 972, Daisies – 473, Tulips – 554, Sunflowers – 576,** and **Asters – 327**. Select the cells containing data and insert a chart on the Excel spreadsheet. Save the spreadsheet as **PP04-E02-FlowerData-[FirstInitialLastName]**. Copy the chart and paste it onto the PowerPoint slide. Change the chart type in PowerPoint to best display the data. Apply chart elements, chart style, chart layout, and color to maintain a high level of readability.

Create a third slide with the title **Garden Health** and insert a SmartArt graphic appropriate for displaying these sequential steps: **Repel Bugs, Replenish Soil, Eliminate Weeds, Provide Water, Check Daily**. Format the SmartArt so it is attractive and easy to read.

You will be evaluated based on the inclusion of all elements specified, your ability to follow directions, your ability to apply newly learned skills to a real-world situation, your creativity, and your demonstration of an entrepreneurial spirit. Submit your final file based on the guidelines provided by your instructor.

Transfer Your Skills

In the course of working through the Transfer Your Skills exercises, you will use critical-thinking and creativity skills to complete the assigned projects using skills taught in the lesson. To evaluate your mastery and completion of the exercises, your instructor may use a rubric, with which more points are allotted according to performance characteristics. (The more you do, the more you earn!) Ask your instructor how your work will be evaluated.

PP04-T01 Use the Web as a Learning Tool

Throughout this book, you will be provided with an opportunity to use the Internet as a learning tool by completing WebQuests. According to the original creators of WebQuests, as described on their website (WebQuest.org), a WebQuest is "an inquiry-oriented activity in which most or all of the information used by learners is drawn from the web." To complete the WebQuest projects in this book, navigate to the student resource center and choose the WebQuest for the lesson on which you are currently working. The subject of each WebQuest will be relevant to the material found in the lesson.

WebQuest Subject: Using Different Chart Types

Submit your final file(s) based on the guidelines provided by your instructor.

PP04-T02 Demonstrate Proficiency

Stormy BBQ is displaying the results of a customer survey on their in-house television screens. New surveys have come in, and the data must be updated. Additionally, many customers report that the current survey results are hard to read.

Open **PP04-T02-BBQ** from the **PP2013 Lesson 04** folder and save it as **PP04-T02-BBQ-[FirstInitialLastName]**. Edit the chart data, after repairing the link, to indicate that 2 kids like the prices, 3 kids like the service, 115 kids like the ribs, 110 adults like the ribs, and 80 adults like the prices.

Apply an appropriate design theme to the presentation. Enlarge and format the chart, hiding/showing chart elements as necessary. Ensure that the chart is attractive and easy to read. On a third slide, create a SmartArt graphic that displays the top three reasons why people love Stormy's.

Submit your final file based on the guidelines provided by your instructor.

Index

Notes

Notes

Notes

Notes

Notes

Notes

Notes

Notes

Notes

Notes